WESLEY AND METHODIST STUDIES

VOLUME I

Edited by
Geordan Hammond
and
David Rainey

DIDSBURY PRESS
MANCHESTER • UK

2009

A publication of the Manchester Wesley Research Centre
in association with
Didsbury Press
Dene Road, Didsbury,
Manchester,
M20 2GU, UK

© Wesley and Methodist Studies

First published 2009

ISBN 978-0-9552507-1-2

CONTENTS

PREFACE

Wesley and Methodist Studies is aimed at making available recent research in the field. It is published through the support of the Manchester Wesley Research Centre, which promotes research in the life and work of John and Charles Wesley, their contemporaries in the eighteenth-century Evangelical Revival, their historical and theological antecedents, their successors in the Wesleyan tradition, and contemporary scholarship in the Wesleyan and Evangelical tradition. This collection of essays will be of importance to scholars and appeal to anyone interested in the broad field covered by this volume.

It is anticipated that *Wesley and Methodist Studies* will be published annually. Prospective authors may submit articles to the editors at any time. Submissions should be sent by email attachment in MS Word. Details on submission guidelines and formatting can be consulted by visiting the web address given below.

The editors would like to thank Didsbury Press for facilitating the publication of this volume, formatting work, and cover design.

Manchester Wesley Research Centre
Attn: Geordan Hammond and David Rainey
Dene Road, Didsbury,
Manchester, M20 2GU,
UK

Email: ghammond@nazarene.ac.uk
Web: http://www.mwrc.ac.uk/wesley-and-methodist-studies/

A MAN OF REASON AND RELIGION?
JOHN WESLEY AND THE ENLIGHTENMENT

Henry D. Rack

In the late Professor J.H. Plumb's *History of England in the Eighteenth Century* there is a lively and provocative chapter on 'John Wesley and the Road to Salvation.' On Methodism's general character Plumb is at first distinctly complimentary and offers some perceptive insights. Methodism had a role as a 'social force for good works.' It appealed because it 'contained so much that was capable of satisfying the deepest needs of human nature' and, unlike the church of its day, 'touched the inner tragedy of man.' As well as emotional release it gave 'a sense of purpose and a field for the exercise of both will and power.' But Plumb continued with a devastating indictment of what he saw as Methodist obscurantism and credulity. 'There was nothing intellectual about Methodism; the rational attitude, the most fashionable intellectual attitude of the day, was absolutely absent.' Wesley believed in witches and demon-possession. He made decisions 'by opening the Bible at random and obeying whatever commands he might discover from the first word which met his eye.' His 'superstitions were those of his uneducated audiences.' His book on medicine was 'an absurd, fantastic compilation of uncritical folklore.' Wesley's notion of education was simply to instil religion and fit children for labour.[1]

If this attack seems excessive and unfair, it must be recognized that Wesley's contemporaries and later critics voiced similar suspicions.[2] Such criticisms, indeed, contain important insights ignored or played down by those who have liked to dwell on Wesley's 'enlightened' intellectual and social concerns as well as his religious insights.[3] He has been portrayed as an empiricist disciple of John Locke, as a modernizing advocate of electric shock therapy in medicine, as a social reformer. More generally, there have been arguments about whether Methodism was a modernizing or reactionary movement. In politics, for example, there have been recurring claims that Methodism 'helped to save England from revolution'—seen as reactionary especially by left-wing historians.[4] But others have claimed that Wesley, despite his self-confessed 'Toryism', created a movement whose spiritual values of liberty, equality, and fraternity unintentionally helped to create secular liberal and reforming movements.[5]

Although some have portrayed Wesley as credulous and superstitious, it has also been common to see Methodism and evangelicalism more sympathetically as an understandable and justifiable 'reaction' of 'vital religion' against what has traditionally been seen as the corrupt, over-rationalistic, sub-Christian state of the Church of England. This also implies that evangelicalism, including Methodism, was in opposition to the Enlightenment.

But what was 'The Enlightenment'? A generation ago it was often seen as a clear, unitary, uniform phenomenon. It expressed a 'desire for human affairs to be guided by rationality rather than faith, superstition or rev-

---

1. J.H. Plumb, *England in the Eighteenth Century* (Harmondsworth, 1950), 94-95.

2. Henry D. Rack, *Reasonable Enthusiast: John Wesley and the Rise of Methodism*, 3rd edn. (Peterborough, 2002), 275-81.

3. Survey and references to recent work in David Hempton, *Methodism: Empire of the Spirit* (New Haven and London, 2005), 41-42, 233-34 notes 14, 15. Older laudatory treatments include George Eayrs, *John Wesley: Christian Philosopher and Church Founder* (London, 1926) and J. Wesley Bready, *England Before and After Wesley* (London, 1938) on social reform.

4. W.E.H. Lecky, *A History of England in the Eighteenth Century*, new ed. (London, 1892), 3:145-46; E. Halevy, *A History of England in 1815*, ET (Penguin ed., London , 1937), 3:47-80; E.P. Thompson, *The Making of the English Working Class*, rev. ed. (Harmondsworth, 1968), 385-440.

5. Bernard Semmel, *The Methodist Revolution* (London, 1974). Despite the title Semmel really argues for Methodist influence on non-violent liberal reforms.

elation; a world view based on science and not tradition.'[6] French attitudes were taken to be typical, notably the anti-church and anti-Christian attitudes of people like Voltaire and Diderot. The tone was neatly captured in the sub-titles of an influential survey in the 1960s: 'The Rise of Modern Paganism' and 'The Science of Freedom'.[7] If there are elements of truth in this portrayal, more recent research has emphasized that the Enlightenment consisted of 'a series of interlocking, and sometimes warring problems and debates.' Its character differed markedly in different national contexts. The relationship between 'enlightenment' and religion and the churches involved compromise and collaboration as well as confrontation.[8]

This was especially true of England.[9] There were, indeed, minorities of outright sceptics and deists at one end of the intellectual spectrum, and anti-intellectual 'enthusiasts' at the other. Yet much more common in mainstream Anglicanism was belief in biblical revelation and church tradition, combined with rational theological reflection on 'Nature's God'. The established church continued to be a central element in national and local society.[10] The older, hostile accounts of the Church of England were influenced by high church, evangelical, and nineteenth century reformist prejudices. More sympathetic and archive-based research suggests a much more nuanced picture of its condition and performance.[11] Educated attitudes towards miracles and providence also turn out to be less purely rationalistic than has been assumed. It had always been acknowledged that the lower orders continued to be influenced by folklore and magic but the degree and

---

6. Dorinda Outram, *The Enlightenment*, 2nd edn. (Cambridge, 2005), 3.

7. Peter Gay, *The Enlightenment. An Interpretation*, 2 vols. (London, 1967, 1970).

8. Outram, *The Enlightenment*, 2; Roy Porter and Mikulas Teich, (eds.) *The Enlightenment in National Context*, (Cambridge, 1981).

9. Porter and Teich, 1-18; Roy Porter, *Enlightenment: Britain and the Creation of the Modern World*, (Harmondsworth, 2001).

10. J.C.D. Clark, *English Society, 1689-1832* (Cambridge, 1985). Though his claim that England was a 'confessional state' seems to overstate Anglican hegemony, there is now a substantial consensus that religion and the established church were significant forces in civic society.

11. Examples are John Walsh, Colin Haydon, and Stephen Taylor, (eds.) *The Church of England, c.1689- c.1833: From Toleration to Tractarianism* (Cambridge, 1993); Jeremy Gregory and J.S. Chamberlain, (eds.), *The National Church in Local Perspective: The Church of England and the Regions, 1660-1800* (Woodbridge, 2003).

nature of the decline in such interests among the more educated after 1700 now seems to have been exaggerated.[12]

Thus the contrast between 'enlightened' and 'evangelical' mentalities now seems less marked and has been eroded further by, for example, David Bebbington's influential study of evangelicalism in Britain. He sees it as having been partly shaped by changing cultural environments which for the eighteenth century means certain 'enlightened' values. They include 'empiricism', the appeal to 'experience' and 'facts'; hostility to the complex, hair-splitting scholastic theology of the seventeenth century; the pursuit of happiness as well as holiness; and a tendency to optimism about the progress of God's kingdom on earth. Wesley figures significantly in Bebbington's presentation (and arguably more obviously than some other evangelicals).[13]

These new perspectives provide a fresh context for assessing Wesley's relationship to the 'enlightened' attitudes of his day.[14] Recent work on his *Primitive Physick* and on his attitude to the supernatural, especially in the light of a less severely rationalistic view of Anglican mentalities, can make him appear closer to mainstream Anglicanism than has often been assumed. The flexibility detected in contemporary Anglicanism by Jeremy Gregory and others also makes Wesley's irregular activities look less un-Anglican and less eccentric than they have often appeared.[15]

---

12. See the influential view on post-1700 rationalising in Keith Thomas, *Religion and the Decline of Magic*, Penguin ed. (Harmondsworth, 1973), chapter XXII; contrast Owen Davies, *Witchcraft, Magic and Culture, 1736-1951* (Manchester, 1999); Jane Shaw, *Miracles in Enlightenment England* (New Haven and London, 2006).

13. David Bebbington, *Evangelicalism in Modern Britain: A History from the 1730s to the 1980s* (London, 1989), 50-60.

14. For Wesley studies seen in the context of modern treatments of the eighteenth century see the introduction to Jeremy Gregory, (ed.) *John Wesley: Tercentenary Essays, Bulletin of the John Rylands University Library of Manchester*, 85:2-3 (Spring and Autumn, 2003), 17-29.

15. Deborah Madden, 'Pristine Purity: Primitivism and Practical Piety in John Wesley's Art of Physic', D.Phil. Thesis (Oxford University, 2003) and '"Experience and the common interest of mankind": the enlightened empiricism of John Wesley's *Primitive Physick*', *British Journal for Eighteenth Century Studies* 26 (2003), 41-54; Robert Webster, 'Methodism and the miraculous: John Wesley's contribution to the Historia Miraculorum', D.Phil. Thesis (Oxford University, 2006); Jeremy Gregory, '"In the Church I will live and die": John Wesley, the Church of England and Methodism' in William Gibson and Robert Ingram, (eds.) *Religious Identities in Britain, 1688-1832* (Ashgate, 2005), 147-78.

Wesley certainly liked to portray himself as 'a man of reason' as well as 'religion' and appealed to 'men of reason and religion' in his writings.[16] He had read deists like Matthew Tindal and William Wollaston and other writers commonly associated with the Enlightenment such as Locke, Shaftesbury, Bernard de Mandeville, Jean-Jacques Rousseau and Francis Hutcheson as well as apologists like George Berkeley and Joseph Butler.[17] He condemned Voltaire and David Hume as 'infidels' and, although it is unclear how well he was acquainted with their writings, he had read some of Hume's Scottish critics.[18] Wesley's qualifications for pursuing subjects other than philosophy may admittedly be questioned. His early biographer John Hampson thought he lacked the ability to pursue science in depth and the more sympathetic Dr John Whitehead acknowledged that he used second-hand sources for science.[19]

Writing to a colleague Wesley claimed that 'Passion and prejudice govern the world, only under the name of reason. It is our part, by religion and reason joined, to counteract them all we can.'[20] This essay attempts to explore how far Wesley fulfilled this ideal and responded positively to what may be regarded as 'The Enlightenment'.

Reason, Empiricism, and the 'Spiritual Senses'

'Reason' was one of the commonest catchwords of the eighteenth century, used not only by notorious sceptics but also by devotional and mystical writers like William Law who influenced Wesley as a young man. In a sermon on 'The Case of Reason Impartially Considered' Wesley praises reason as not only of great use in the things of this life but also for 'laying the foundations

---

16. For example, 'An Earnest Appeal to Men of Reason and Religion' and sequels (1743-45) in *The Appeals to Men of Reason and Religion*, vol. 11 of the Bicentennial Edition of the Works of John Wesley (hereinafter BE), ed. Gerald R. Cragg (Oxford, 1975).

17. See the early reading list in V.H.H. Green, *The Young Mr Wesley* (London, 1961), Appendix I, 305-19; for other examples cited see the index to *Journals and Diaries*, vols. 18-24 of BE Works of John Wesley, ed. W.R. Ward and R.P. Heitzenrater.

18. *Journals*, BE, 23:121; 22:172.

19. John Hampson, *Memoirs of John Wesley*, 3 vols. (Sunderland, 1791), 3:175-76; John Whitehead, *Life of John Wesley... and Charles Wesley*, 2 vols. (London, 1794-96), 2:465.

20. John Wesley to Joseph Benson, 5 October 1770 in *The Letters of John Wesley, A.M.*, ed. John Telford, 8 vols. (London, 1931), 5:203.

of true religion, under the guidance of the Spirit of God' and even for 'raising the superstructure'. Faith is always consistent with reason, although reason cannot produce faith. This requires a higher sense.[21]

What is striking and in accord with contemporary intellectual assumptions is that Wesley's view of the sources of knowledge is strongly empiricist. He denies that we have any innate ideas: our knowledge comes solely through the senses and reflection on the information they convey. This is the opposite to the type of rationalism dependent on innate ideas common in the seventeenth century. Where did Wesley acquire this stance? It has been common to attribute it to the influence of John Locke and more especially to Peter Browne. [22] Wesley certainly studied both thinkers, though with some criticisms, but recent research suggests that he owed more to his education in the Oxford Aristotelian tradition.[23] Whatever its source, Wesley's empiricism clearly coloured his approach to a variety of subjects. On science he professed only to describe the appearance of things and thought some of Isaac Newton's ideas were too speculative![24] On medicine he disclaimed elaborate theories in favour of simply endorsing what worked.[25] Although, as we shall see, he repeated stories of apparitions and poltergeists from seventeenth-century writers as matters of fact, he dismissed their attempts to offer quasi-scientific 'explanations' of such things.[26]

This severe empiricism and refusal to speculate on underlying causes Wesley extended to theology. It is remarkable that so orthodox a man in a century when there was much questioning of the doctrine of the Trinity, while asserting that the doctrine is a 'fact' on the evidence of Scripture, nev-

---

21. Sermon on 'The Case of Reason' in *Sermons*, vols. 1-4 of BE, ed. Albert Outler (Nashville, 1984-87), 2:593.' Reason 'Wesley defines as a 'faculty of the soul' exercised in 'apprehension', 'judgement' and 'discourse', 2:590.

22. For example by Richard E. Brantley, *Locke, Wesley and the Method of English Romanticism* (Gainesville, FL, 1984).

23. Rex Matthews, '"Reason and Religion Joined": A Study in the Theology of John Wesley', D. Theol. diss. (Harvard University, 1986); Mark T. Mealey, 'Tilting at Windmills: John Wesley's reading of John Locke's epistemology', in *John Wesley, Tercentenary Essays*, 331-46.

24. John Wesley, *Works*, 14 vols. (London, 1872), 14:300-303; *Journal*, BE, 21:81-82; 22:24, 215-16.

25. John Wesley, *Primitive Physick*, 24th edn. (London, 1792), Preface, paragraphs 7, 8, 11, 13 and see note 15 above.

26. *Journal*, BE, 20:401; 22:135-36, 178.

ertheless refused to speculate on any particular *explanation* of the words 'Father', 'Son' and 'Holy Ghost'. He would not even insist on using the terms 'Trinity' and 'Person'.[27]

What he *did* try to do was to extend the notion of knowledge given purely through the senses to religious experience and salvation. As already noted, he did not believe that reason by itself could bring salvation nor could knowledge derived from the normal senses. Spiritual knowledge comes through 'spiritual senses': 'a new class of senses opened in your soul, not dependent on organs of flesh and blood' to be 'the evidence of things not seen' as bodily senses are of visible things. This is a gift of God and not a natural endowment but opened up by faith.[28] It should be emphasized that people like Locke and Browne did not allow for any such sense—when Locke talked about things 'above reason' he meant things known only from the written revelation of the Bible.[29] Wesley's 'spiritual sense' is a personalized gift of God by the Holy Spirit. He also believed that assurance of salvation comes from the same source along with the practical evidence of a changed life. Similarly, he saw our 'moral sense' or 'conscience' as a special gift of God and not, like contemporary philosophers, as a 'natural' attribute. Yet he was at least attempting to make spiritual, like all other knowledge, be conveyed through a kind of 'sense' channel.[30]

Theological Simplification and the Way of Salvation

Protestant theology since the Reformation and especially in the seventeenth century had been developed into intricate scholastic 'systems' full of fine-drawn definitions, distinctions, and technical jargon. In the eighteenth century there was a revulsion from this in favour of simpler, more moral, more rational, and indeed more exclusively biblical teaching.[31] Although this could

---

27. *Sermons*, BE, 4:376-78.

28. *Appeals*, BE, 11:56-57, compare 11:46 on faith.

29. John Locke, *Essay on Human Understanding*, IV:xvii:23; Brantley, *Locke, Wesley*, 32-35, mistakenly implies that Locke and Browne allowed for direct divine communications like Wesley. See H.D. Rack, 'Wesley and Romanticism', in *Proceedings of the Wesley Historical Society*, xlv (1985), 63-65.

30. See Wesley's criticism of Francis Hutcheson in his sermon 'On Conscience' in *Sermons*, BE, 3:483-84.

31. John Locke, *Reasonableness of Christianity* (1695) reduced theology to a few essentials with

lead to anti-Trinitarianism and outright scepticism and deism this was not necessarily so. Some evangelicals, especially Calvinists, still used the scholastic categories in controversy but Wesley increasingly did not.

Unlike most evangelicals he was also aggressively anti-Calvinist, an Arminian like most eighteenth-century Anglicans. What is more, he became a more and more open-minded and tolerant 'evangelical' as he grew older. At Oxford he had been a rigid high churchman; for a time after his 1738 conversion an equally rigid 'salvation by faith through conversion' man. But he never really lost sight of his early vision of holiness, even what he called 'perfection', as the goal of the Christian life. In 1746 he described the main Methodist beliefs as repentance, faith, and holiness: the first is the 'porch', the second the 'door', the third 'religion itself'.[32] In the 1760s he allowed that you could be justified regardless of the particular language and formulas used, even that a man like William Law who denied justification by faith could have it.[33] In 1770 he outraged Calvinist evangelicals by dismissing disputes on 'merit' as hair-splitting and useless.[34] Elsewhere he said that faith is not the end but the means. 'The end of the commandment is love. Let this love be attained, by whatever means, and I am content.'[35] His talk of perfection and claim that without good works we could not ultimately be saved outraged other evangelicals. Yet he was always careful to say that ultimately we all depend on Christ and grace for salvation.

Toleration

Religious toleration has been regarded by most Christians for most of Christian history as a vice rather than a virtue. Catholics and Protestants alike persecuted deviants even to death. The seventeenth century saw limited beginnings of toleration, though without full civil equality, in England from 1689. Wesley was clearly affected by the increase of the tolerant spirit which can

---

much biblical citation. Richard Watson, as professor of divinity at Cambridge, drew only on the Bible and common sense for theology: R. Watson, *Anecdotes*, (London, 1818), 1:62 and following.

32. Wesley, *Letters*, ed. Telford, 2:268.

33. *Journals*, BE, 22:114-15.

34. Discussed, with references, in Rack, *Reasonable Enthusiast*, 459-60.

35. Wesley, *Letters*, vol. 26 of BE, ed. Frank Baker, 26:203.

be seen among his educated contemporaries. In a very eighteenth-century manner he claimed that the very foundation of a person's religion is 'private judgement'. The Reformation could never have taken place but for 'the right of private judgement on which the whole Reformation stands.' Liberty of conscience is a right 'by the law of God and nature as well as of England'.[36] This is certainly an 'Enlightenment' value and very different from earlier Protestantism.

In principle, too, Wesley was remarkably tolerant of how far Christians can legitimately differ. 'Right opinion is at best but a very slender part of religion (which properly and directly consists in right tempers, words and actions) and frequently no part of religion at all.' By 'opinions' he meant 'whatever is consistent with a love of Christ and a work of grace.' So in his sermon on 'The Catholic Spirit' he allows that if people agree on basic Christianity they can tolerate many differences on matters such as church order, ministry, and worship.[37] There were, indeed, limitations on these ideals in practice. Though Wesley was utterly opposed to physical persecution and recognized that Roman Catholics could be saved despite their wrong 'opinions', he shared traditional English prejudices against them as disloyal and persecuting, so he opposed granting them full civil rights. He frequently attacked Calvinists because he saw predestination as dishonouring God and undermining aspirations to holiness. Though his formula of agreement on essentials and toleration of diversity in other matters is an attractive one, problems arose when he found that what he saw as an 'opinion' was for others basic to true Christianity, like believer's baptism for Baptists.[38]

36. Wesley, *Letters*, ed. Telford, 4:151-52; *Journal*, BE, 19:320; Sermon on 'The Catholic Spirit', BE, 2:86; *Letters*, ed. Telford, 5:22.

37. Wesley, *Letters*, ed. Telford, 4:347 compare 3:203; Sermon 'On the Trinity', BE, 2:374-76; *Letters*, ed. Telford 4:297; Sermon 'On the Catholic Spirit', BE, 2:81-95. On precedents for Wesley's distinction see Stephen Sykes, 'The Fundamentals of Christianity', in Stephen Sykes and John Booty, (eds.) *The Study of Anglicanism* (London, 1988), 231-44.

38. For Wesley's views on Roman Catholics and attacks on Calvinism see Rack, *Reasonable Enthusiast*, 305-13, 198-202, 450-61. For the baptism problem see, *Letters*, BE, 26:425 against Gilbert Boyce, 26:420-21.

Education

Professor Plumb was mistaken to dismiss Wesley's views on education as narrow and exploitative. He was actively in favour of male and female education on quite generous lines and certainly had no bias against educating the poor. Indeed in this respect he seems more 'enlightened' than some Enlightenment leaders who thought the lower orders would be more dutiful if kept in thrall to the religion despised by their betters.[39]

Wesley supported schools founded by his followers and the Sunday School movement. His Kingswood school was a kind of grammar school with aspirations to add an academic course he claimed would be more effective than for most attending Oxford and Cambridge! The school aimed to produce 'rational, scriptural Christians' through a fairly conventional classical course with some modern subjects and religious training. He condemned contemporary genteel female education as offensive to any intelligent woman since it treated them as designed only to be 'agreeable playthings.' [40]

But in some basic principles Wesley differed sharply from Enlightenment views of education which tended to see human nature as basically good unless perverted by priest-craft and superstition. This could be countered by the right kind of education. But for Wesley we are fallen creatures and only saved by the grace of God. 'All our wisdom will not make them [children] understand, much less *feel* the things of God.' Yet because he respects the power of reason and the impact of sense-impressions, education has an important role in cultivating mental, moral, and religious development. 'The bias of nature is set the wrong way. Education is designed to set it right.' It restores our rational nature, it is 'reason learned at second-hand, which is, as far as it can, to supply the loss of original perfection.'[41]

Moreover, Wesley's voluminous writings and abridgements of others' works, his *Journal* and *Arminian Magazine* were used as vehicles for educating his followers on many subjects in addition to religion: science, history,

---

39. Peter Gay, *The Enlightenment*, 2:517-28.

40. See the survey in my chapter in Joy A. Palmer (ed.), *Fifty Major Thinkers in Education*, 2 vols. (London, 2001), 1:50-55. 'Agreeable playthings': sermon on 'Visiting the Sick', BE, 3:396.

41. Wesley, *Letters*, ed. Telford, 6:39; 'A Thought on the Manner of Educating Children' in Wesley, *Works* (1872), 13:476 echoing Milton; Sermon 'On the Education of Children', BE, 3:348 quoting William Law.

travel, scenery, and architecture. In these matters he reflected contemporary educated taste. Thus he disliked the 'horrid mountains' of the Pennines and Derbyshire Peak, preferring cultivated landscapes. He liked to moralize that those who lavished money on mansions went bankrupt or did not live to enjoy them.[42]

Political and Social Concerns

In politics, Enlightenment ideas have been credited with influencing the 'democratic' American and French Revolutions. But there was also the controlling paternalism of the so-called 'enlightened despots.' Wesley was opposed to democracy either in the state or in Methodism. He attacked the American rebels and radicals in England. He claimed to be a 'Tory', defined as on who sees God and not the people as the source of political authority.[43]

In social matters he was more 'enlightened' though with some ambiguities. Keen on charity, both individual and through voluntary organizations, he ran collections for the poor, aid for work, and medical help. He also supported the anti-slave trade campaign. His 'Use of Money' sermon taught: 'Gain all you can, save all you can, give all you can', the first two points being only to support the third. He distrusted the rich and was tender towards the poor, not blaming them for their plight. This was uncommon in his day— 'enlightened' and evangelical charity often involved oversight and discrimination. Wesley behaved more like an old-style Catholic in his unconditional giving.[44]

Wesley also shared a type of eighteenth-century optimism about social progress. He echoed mainstream contemporary religious belief that before Christ's Second Coming there would be a period of progress on earth

---

42.   See W.R. Ward on Wesley's *Journals*, BE, 18:62-68 (Introduction); on stately homes, e.g. *Journal*, BE, 21:147.

43.   On Enlightenment politics see Outram, 28-46, 134-37; Wesley, *Letters*, ed. Telford, 7:305-306; and the discussion of Wesley's politics in Rack, *Reasonable Enthusiast*, 270-80.

44.   Sermon on 'The Use of Money', BE, 2:263-80; discussion of Wesley's social views in Rack, *Reasonable Enthusiast*, 360-70; John Walsh, 'John Wesley and the Community of Goods', in *Protestant Evangelicalism: Britain, Ireland, Germany and America c1750-c1950: Essays in Honour of W.R. Ward*, Studies in Church History, Subsidia 7, ed. Keith Robbins (London, 1990), 25-50.

including the spread of the gospel which encouraged missionary endeavour (curiously, Charles Wesley was more pessimistic and indulged in calculations about the date of the End on the basis of the book of 'Revelation').[45]

Voluntary Associations and Church Order

In his recent study of *Methodism: Empire of the Spirit*, David Hempton claims that Wesley and Methodism reflect Enlightenment values in at least two ways. One is the empiricist view of knowledge already discussed. The other is more unusual and has been little studied in these terms: what Hempton sees as a voluntary style of church order.[46] England was notable in this period for its culture of clubs and voluntary organizations.[47] They included various religious societies which became a characteristic feature of evangelicalism in England and elsewhere. Wesley had experimented with a variety of religious associations and liked to portray Methodism as simply a religious society and not a church. He saw it as open to all, though also as an auxiliary to the Church of England. Perhaps, since he saw himself as running a voluntary society and not a church, he felt freer to experiment and devise his own rules. Yet in doing so he was unwittingly organizing a religious body on ecclesiastical principles quite different from those of most existing English churches. Answering a critic of his violations of Anglican order Wesley wrote: 'What is the end of all ecclesiastical order? Is it not to bring souls from the power of Satan to God? And to build them up in his fear and love? Order, then, is so far valuable as it answers these ends. And if it answers them not it is nothing worth.' 'Where the knowledge and love of God are, true order will not be wanting.' Already in the 1740s Wesley supported a very minimal defini-

---

45. Sermon on 'The General Spread of the Gospel', BE, 2:485-99. Evangelical millenarianism: Bebbington, 63-67, 81-86; W.R.Ward, *Early Evangelicalism: A Global Intellectual History, 1690-1789* (Cambridge, 2006), 119-39; for Charles Wesley, Kenneth Newport, 'Charles Wesley's Interpretation of some Biblical Prophecies', *Bulletin of the John Rylands University Library* 77 (1995), 31-52.

46. Hempton, 50-52, drawing on Frederick Dreyer, *The Genesis of Methodism*, (Bethlehem, NJ, 1999), 93, 96-105.

47. Peter Clark, *British Clubs and Societies, 1580-1800: The Origins of an Associational World* (Oxford, 2000). Unfortunately, Clark chose to say little on religious associations.

tion of the Church of England and ignored the whole issue of its status as an established church. Establishment he once described as a 'merely political institution.'[48]

Hempton sees Wesley as in effect applying an Enlightenment 'principle of consent in natural jurisprudence' to church order. That is to say, a conception based 'not upon apostolic authority, confessional orthodoxy, or state coercion but rather on the free consent of equals to form a voluntary association.'[49] Hence Wesley's rule-making and pragmatic creation of informal ministries of men and women as leaders and preachers. If Wesley was half-consciously effecting a new kind of church order based on adapting means to the demands of the gospel, two caveats are in order in response to Hempton's characterization of it. One is that when Wesley did create a formal church for America he adapted a form of threefold ministry which he thought was justified by antiquity. Secondly, although Wesley liked to portray his organization as originating in people voluntarily asking him to lead them, he ruled it autocratically. You were free to differ from him, but if so you had to leave![50] There were periodic complaints and secessions about this.

Wesley and the Supernatural

So far we have seen that a plausible case can be made for Wesley having shared some of the values often associated with the Enlightenment. But in his attitude to the supernatural he seems to depart most decisively from it, not only from deists and sceptics but also from moderate mainstream Anglicans who combined reason with acceptance of the biblical revelation. Such people saw God as creating and upholding the world. While accepting the truth of biblical miracles they did not expect God to act in this way in later times, though it was not denied that he could do so.[51]

Wesley often seemed to go well beyond this position. Not only did he allow for direct, contemporary intervention by God in the lives of

---

48. *Letters,* BE, 26:205-206. For Conference discussions of church order see Rack, *Reasonable Enthusiast,* 293-94.

49. Hempton, 51.

50. For the American scheme and Wesley's authoritarianism see Rack, *Reasonable Enthusiast,* 507-26, 246-48.

51. For Anglican attitudes to miracles see Shaw, *Miracles.*

Methodists but also was fascinated by, and publicized, apparently super-natural events. Protestants generally believed that miracles had ceased either with the end of the apostles or at least after the time of Constantine. Later claims to miracles by Roman Catholics or eccentric Protestant enthusiasts were generally dismissed as frauds or delusions.[52] Wesley confronted the is-sue most directly in his critique of Conyers Middleton's *Free Inquiry into the Miraculous Powers which are supposed to have existed in the Christian Church* (1749). Middleton's claim to discredit miracles alleged since the apostles' time was ostensibly directed against Roman Catholics, but most readers, like Wesley, suspected it was also intended to undermine biblical miracles. Wes-ley was prepared to believe miracles possible until Constantine's day after which the power was lost, partly because it was no longer needed to support Christianity, and partly because of the growth of corruption in the church. Wesley took the orthodox contemporary view that the 'external' evidences of Christianity supporting Christ's claim to a divine mission include fulfilled prophecy and miracles. But he conceded that external evidences may lose cogency through time and that God may have allowed this to happen so that the 'internal evidence' of religious experience, which is always fresh and con-temporary, would have more force.[53]

Early Methodists seemed to claim the same kind of sudden conver-sions and charismatic phenomena as in apostolic times. Wesley liked to as-sert that they were not claiming special or extraordinary gifts but only those open to all Christians now as then. Many of his respectable contemporaries thought he was wrong and that grace through baptism followed by religious nurture is all that can now be expected. Moreover, it was suspected that Wes-ley and his followers were claiming more direct, personalized, and special blessings. In Wesley's *Journal* and Methodist autobiographies there were claims to 'particular providences'—special interventions to save believers as well as lurid 'judgements' on opponents. Rain apparently stopped when Wesley preached; demon-possession and exorcism were recorded and Wes-ley notoriously believed in the reality of witchcraft. He published many ac-counts of them and of poltergeists and apparitions as 'facts'. He believed such

---

52. Yet Protestant 'providences' seemed very similar: Shaw, *Miracles*, 30-32.
53. Wesley, *Letters*, ed. Telford, 2:312-88; internal evidences 2:383-85.

things as recorded in the Bible, attested by reliable witnesses and accepted by wise men in all ages except the sceptics of his own day.[54]

Moreover, despite his denials, there were grounds for suspecting that he felt that Methodism and his leadership of it were divinely commissioned and blessed. He had a strong sense of 'calling' and providential guidance. He saw his preachers (including some women) as the subjects of an 'extraordinary call'. In 1760 he wrote to Charles Wesley: 'I care not a rush for ordinary means, only that it is our duty to try them. All our lives and all God's dealing with us have been extraordinary from the beginning…I have been preternaturally restored more than ten times.'[55]

Conclusion

In the light of the issues discussed in this paper, it seems fair to say that Professor Plumb's implied dismissal of any connection of Wesley to the Enlightenment was exaggerated and in some respects misleading. Recent studies of the Enlightenment and of the character of contemporary English religion suggest that Wesley was nearer than has often been allowed to the centre of a spectrum stretching from deists and sceptics at one end to claimants to divine inspiration at the other.

Yet doubts remain. Professor Kent questions Wesley's apparent empiricism and claims to be a rational analyst of the religious experiences of his followers as evidence of the truth of his message. Arguably, he too readily claimed divine and supernatural explanations and did not consider naturalistic ones with sufficient open-mindedness.[56] Interestingly, Charles Wesley criticized John's credulity about Methodist claims to conversion and perfection.[57] Alexander Knox, who knew Wesley well in old age, perceptively commented on his theology and personality. Wesley 'would have been an enthusiast if he could' but 'there was a firmness in his intellectual texture which

---

54. Examples and discussion in W.R. Ward's Introduction to *Journal*, BE, 18:49-52; Rack, *Reasonable Enthusiast*, 431-35, 439-40; see Webster, 'Methodism and the Miraculous', for sympathetic appraisal.

55. Wesley, *Letters*, ed. Telford, 4:108, 162; 5:257.

56. John Kent, *Wesley and the Wesleyans* (Cambridge, 2002), 37-40.

57. My essay on 'Charles Wesley and the Supernatural' will appear in a forthcoming *Bulletin of the John Rylands University Library of Manchester* edited by Robert Webster.

would not bend to illusion.' Yet while Knox was trying to distance Wesley from the wild visionaries of the mid-seventeenth century he admitted that he was prone to find supernatural explanations where natural ones were more plausible.[58] It might be said that although Wesley asserted that knowledge comes only through the senses, his 'spiritual senses' were only 'empirical' in form.

It is nevertheless important as well as fair to see why he was so keen to invoke supernatural and divine intervention. He was attempting to counter the threat of contemporary scepticism, and here he was tackling a fundamental issue with huge implications for the future. Hence, he said, he wrote on science and history to 'bring God into them'. Any case of witchcraft or demonic possession defeated the sceptics because it disproved their assumption that the universe was closed to supernatural intervention. He charged sceptics with trying to treat morality and conscience as purely 'natural' endowments, 'not suffering even the being of a God.'[59]

David Hempton portrays Wesley and Methodism as 'occupying a position of creative tension between ... enlightenment and enthusiasm.' Hence Methodism 'thrived on the raw edge of religious excitement without, in the main, capitulating to some of the more extreme manifestations of popular religion.'[60] On Wesley himself Hempton concludes, nevertheless, that Wesley was, 'in a peculiar sense, a reasonable enthusiast, but an enthusiast for all that.'[61] That is one way of evaluating the complicated balance between rationality and credulity in Wesley's mind, and I am inclined to agree. Did he really conceal enthusiasm in garments of reasonableness? Others, while recognizing his enthusiasm, will prefer to stress his reasonableness.[62]

58. Knox on Wesley in Robert Southey, *Life of Wesley*, ed. M.H. Fitzgerald, 2 vols. (Oxford , 1925), 2:356-57.

59. Wesley, *Letters*, ed. Telford, 6:67; *Journal*, BE, 22:135-36; Sermon 'On the Unity of the Divine being', BE, 4:67-69.

60. Hempton, 49-50, 52, 54.

61. Hempton, 41.

62. Shaw, *Miracles* ,78-79; Webster, 'Methodism and the Miraculous'.

PNEUMATOLOGY THROUGH CORRESPONDENCE:
THE LETTERS OF JOHN WESLEY
AND 'JOHN SMITH' (1745 – 1748)

Joseph W. Cunningham

From May 1745 to March 1748, John Wesley was engaged in correspondence with a pseudonymous figure named 'John Smith'. Smith's identity remains a mystery, except that he was well versed in theology and, according
to Frank Baker, most likely a clergyman.[1] In the correspondence begun by
Smith, there are twelve letters—six written by himself and six by Wesley. Although the topics of conversation ranged from lay preaching to the possib-
ity of present-day miracles, much of their discussion centred on the issue
of 'perceptible inspiration'—the belief that men and women of faith could
perceive the operations of the Holy Spirit at work in the soul.

Smith's letters were prompted by his reading of Wesley's *An Earnest
Appeal to Men of Reason and Religion* (1743), as well as selections from his
Farther Appeal (1744-45). Baker has commented that, given the time frame
and circumstances, this interest was most likely sparked by a brush with prac-
ticing 'Methodists' in or around the Bristol area.[2] Whatever way he formed
his acquaintance with the revival, Smith came to know of Wesley's teaching

---

1. *Letters II (1740-1755)*, vol. 26 of The Bicentennial Edition of the Works of John Wesley, ed. Frank Baker (Nashville, TN, 1982), 138.

2. *Letters II*, 138.

on the witness of the Spirit, and found it highly problematic. Laying bare his grievance, Smith pressed Wesley for a viable answer to the perplexing question of perceptible inspiration:

> The question then is this, does God's Spirit work perceptibly on our spirit by direct testimony...by such perceivable impulses and dictates as are as distinguishable from the suggestions of our own faculties as light is discernable from darkness...or does he imperceptibly influence our minds to goodness by gently and insensibly assisting our faculties, and biasing them aright?[3]

In other words: Is there such a thing as perceptible or sensible inspiration? Does the Spirit bear a direct witness to believers of their salvation, or does God influence us in an exclusively imperceptible way? This was the question put to Wesley, and it was one that Smith thought deserving of an explanation.

Amidst a busy itinerancy filled with preaching and publication, Wesley accepted the challenge extended him by Smith, and responded to each of his letters with care and precision. In some respects, it seems that the two had met their match in one another. Both men were knowledgeable of the church and her theology, both were well-educated and articulate, both were adept at critically analyzing opposing positions, and both expressed a sincere interest in seeking the truth. After these commonalities, however, harmony ended and dissonance began. Unlike Smith, Wesley embraced the idea of 'perceptible inspiration.' He believed that in the economy of salvation,[4] the Spirit of God offered a direct testimony of faith to human beings. Moreover, he believed that men and women could perceive the inspiration of the Spirit at work on one's soul as the fruits of peace, joy, and love were germinated in the heart. Wesley's high esteem for this teaching can hardly be questioned:

---

3. *Letters II*, 188.

4. Hereafter, the term 'economy' and its variants will be used to express the domain, or realm of the human experience of salvation. In this sense, Wesley's pneumatology is economic and not speculative. In other words, he was concerned to express the Holy Spirit's significance, but only in its relation to human experience and salvation.

'For this [perceptible inspiration] I earnestly contend; and so do all who are called Methodist preachers.'[5]

This essay has two aims. First, it seeks to outline the significance of John Wesley's theology of perceptible inspiration by tracing its dialectical development throughout the Smith/Wesley correspondence. While numerous scholars heretofore have reflected upon the letter exchange, no one has appraised the full extent of Wesley's pneumatological sympathies found therein. Although Randy Maddox in *Responsible Grace* and Kenneth Collins in *Holy Love and the Shape of Grace* have highlighted the doctrine of 'perceptible inspiration' and connected it to Wesley's understanding of the witness and fruits of the Spirit,[6] the broad nature of their respective works curtailed the possibility of in-depth investigation. Surprisingly, perceptible inspiration receives even less attention in Lycurgus Starkey's monograph: *The Work of the Holy Spirit: A Study in Wesleyan Theology*. Though Starkey quotes from the Smith/Wesley correspondence to show that 'perceptibility' is part of the nature of inspiration in Wesley's thinking, he fails in providing a thorough analysis of its pneumatological import.[7] Thus, given the correspondence's overall lack of pneumatological appraisal by contemporaries, this essay aims to analyze perceptible inspiration in its epistolary context to help fill in some gaps in Wesley scholarship.

Second, this essay aims to deal with the question of religious epistemology arising from John Wesley's theology of perceptible inspiration. It has long been supposed that Wesley had adopted some form of empiricism in his consideration of divine knowledge. Rex Matthews and Richard Heitzenrater among others have contributed to this position.[8] Heitzenrater, for instance,

---

5. *Letters II*, 182.

6. See Randy L. Maddox, *Responsible Grace: John Wesley's Practical Theology* (Nashville, TN, 1994), 128-129; and also Kenneth J. Collins, *The Theology of John Wesley: Holy Love and the Shape of Grace* (Nashville, TN, 2007), 142-143.

7. See Lycurgus Starkey, *The Work of the Holy Spirit: A Study in Wesleyan Theology* (Nashville, TN, 1962), 17.

8. Other contributions include Hoo-Jung Lee, 'Experiencing the Spirit in Wesley and Macarius', in *Rethinking Wesley's Theology for Contemporary Methodism*, ed. Randy L. Maddox (Nashville, TN, 1998), 201. Lee contends that one 'of the most prominent features of Wesley's pneumatology is his insistence that the Spirit's gracious work in our lives is perceptible. He explained the possibility of such perception with an empiricist account of *sensus spiritualis*.'

posits that Wesley had adopted a 'generally empirical approach to questions of knowledge. He had quite early settled upon a Lockean approach to matters of this sort.'[9] However, Wesley's correspondence with Smith presents challenges to such a view. As will be suggested in this essay, Wesley's theology of divine knowledge relied upon the more ancient tradition of participation. Stephen Long has argued this view in his book, *John Wesley's Moral Theology: The Quest for God and Goodness*, which provides a convincing alternative to the former.[10]

By accomplishing the above aims, this essay seeks to establish perceptible inspiration as a suitable model for developing a broader understanding of John Wesley's economic pneumatology. While Albert Outler defined it as his 'theory of religious knowledge,'[11] such is much too narrow. More than a religious epistemology, perceptible inspiration embodied Wesley's understanding of the 'way of the Spirit' in the economy of salvation. It is here put forward that Wesley's understanding of perceptible inspiration can best be characterized as his '*via Spiritus*'—or way of the Spirit. Wesley believed that the experience of perceptible inspiration began with God's gracious relationality, which enabled humans to receive the gift of faith. When embraced,

---

9. Richard P. Heitzenrater, *Mirror and Memory: Reflections on Early Methodism* (Nashville, TN, 1989), 109. See also, Henry D. Rack, 'John Wesley and the Enlightenment', unpublished paper (Tyndale Conference, 2005), 3. 'It is now fairly recognized that, at least in philosophical terms, Wesley was an empiricist and his affinity with this and other aspects of the Enlightenment has come to be recognized in varying degrees.' A revised version of this paper will be published in this volume of *Wesley and Methodist Studies*. See also Rex Dale Matthews, '"Religion and Reason Joined": A Study in the Theology of John Wesley', D.Theol. diss. (Harvard University, 1986), 309. While its true that Wesley's philosophy of physical knowledge was based on some form of empiricism, his theology of spiritual knowledge was more akin to the tradition of divine participation—i.e., a knowledge of communion with God, rather than knowledge of spiritually-sensed ideas or propositions.

10. Duane Stephen Long, *John Wesley's Moral Theology: The Quest for God and Goodness* (Nashville, TN, 2005). This theme can also be found in Theodore Runyon, *The New Creation: John Wesley's Theology Today* (Nashville, TN, 1998), 76-77. Runyon claims that Wesley '[relied] on this ancient tradition, but [applied] to it the pattern of Lockean epistemology'. In other words, while the form of Wesley's epistemic theology was empiricist, the substance was wholly other; or as Runyon contended, experience 'mediates access' not to propositions, but to 'participation in, divine reality.'

11. Albert C. Outler, *John Wesley* (New York, 1980), 3.

faith served as our faculty (or epistemic means) for perceiving the testimony of the Spirit, which witnessed the moral fruits of peace, joy, love, and righteousness. A parallel to the *via salutis* (or way of salvation), the *via Spiritus* of perceptible inspiration was crucial for John Wesley's economic pneumatology. Wesley hardly concerned himself with theological conjecture. He was never compelled to wax speculative on the person and operations of the Holy Spirit. Rather, he sought throughout his life to propound the importance of present and final salvation—the ultimate spiritual gift. Perceptible inspiration was fundamental to Wesley's pneumatology precisely for this reason: it encompassed his understanding of the Spirit's way of operation in relation to humanity. The *via Spiritus* reflected Wesley's ongoing conviction that God was intimately present to men and women along the journey of salvation. As such, it provides a suitable model for investigating his theology of the Holy Spirit's work and mission.

Perceptible Inspiration in the 'Smith-Wesley' Correspondence

The doctrine of perceptible inspiration lay at the heart of the Smith-Wesley correspondence. To Wesley as well as Smith, this had quickly become one of the central issues of contention. Wesley espoused it, and Smith challenged it. Summing up the doctrine with a set of rhetorical questions, Wesley stated this to his opponent:

> We are now at length come to the real state of the question between Methodists (so called) and their opponents. Is there perceptible inspiration or is there not? Is there such a thing...as faith producing peace and joy and love, and inward (as well as outward) holiness? Is that faith which is productive of these fruits wrought in us by the Holy Ghost, or not? And is he in whom they are wrought necessarily *conscious* of them, or is he not?[12]

Wesley defined perceptible inspiration as the interconnectivity of faith and its fruits. Peace, joy, and love blossomed in the lives of believers by the work of the Holy Spirit. Faith was the condition, which was appropriated by God's

12. *Letters II*, 183.

gracious gift of relationship. It was, he explained, 'the demonstrative evidence of things unseen, the supernatural evidence of things invisible, not perceivable by eyes of flesh, or by any of our natural senses or faculties.'[13] Analogous to the way in which we needed our natural eyes to see and our ears to hear, humans also needed spiritual eyes and ears (faith) to participate in God's divine life. Those who received this gift were enabled to perceive the witness of the Spirit. Becoming conscious of God's pardoning presence, men and women of faith were imbued a filial confidence and trust in God. This then led to the life of holiness, filled with love for God and neighbour. As Wesley described it, perceptible inspiration was tantamount to one's awareness of the Spirit affecting one's life, as witnessed through the eyes of faith opened by God's grace.

Elsewhere in the correspondence, Wesley lent further nuance to his theology of perceptible inspiration. In the example given below, he characterizes it by the tangible fruits of the Spirit germinated in Christian practice:

> [By perceptible inspiration] We mean that inspiration of God's Holy Spirit whereby he fills us with righteousness, peace, and joy, with love to him and all mankind. And we believe it cannot be, in the nature of things, that a man should be filled with this peace and joy and love by the inspiration of the Holy Ghost without perceiving it, as clearly as he does the light of the sun.[14]

Wesley was adamant that none could be truly Christian without knowing it, that is, without consciously expressing love to humankind based on a personal experience of peace and hope in the Holy Spirit. Though his views on assurance developed over the course of his ministry, still he remained convinced that personal awareness of pardon was essential for the Christian life, though this awareness was not a condition for receiving pardon.[15] For

---

13. *The Appeals to Men of Reason and Religion and Certain Related Open Letters*, vol. 11 of The Bicentennial Edition of the Works of John Wesley, ed. Gerald R. Cragg (Nashville, TN, 1989), 46.

14. *Letters II*, 182.

15. Writing to his brother Charles, John expressed the following sentiment concerning saving faith and assurance: 'It is flatly absurd. For how can a sense of our having received pardon be the condition of receiving it?' *Letters II*, 254-255.

Wesley, being Christian was much more than gaining entrance into heaven. Salvation was a present reality. In his sermon on 'Salvation by Faith' (1738), he explained it as 'something attainable, yea, actually attained here on earth, by those who are partakers of this faith.'[16] Later, in 'The Scripture Way of Salvation' (1765), he affirmed his earlier definition: salvation 'is not [only] what is frequently understood by that word, the going to heaven, eternal happiness'; '[it] is not something at a distance: it is a present thing, a blessing which, through the free mercy of God, ye are now in possession.'[17] Soteriologically, Wesley allowed the provision that one might be justified (and go on to experience final salvation) without receiving the full assurance of faith or witness of the Spirit. Such, initially, was Wesley's personal experience.[18] However, the fullness of *present* salvation was tied to perceptible inspiration. In order to love our neighbour we must love God; but 'this love cannot be in us till we receive the "Spirit of adoption, crying in our hearts, Abba, Father".'[19] Wesley remained convinced that none could fully embrace the Christian life, here and now, without an inward testimony of the Spirit's operation.

Smith received Wesley's pneumatology of perceptible inspiration with disdain. He thought it irrational to suggest that God in Spirit offered a personal, perceptible testimony of salvation to human beings. Based on his experience, such was simply not the case. He believed that God inspired human beings to be sure, but imperceptibly and gradually, that is, as he expressed it, 'by hearing, by hearing the Word of God soberly and consistently explained, and not from any momentous illapse from heaven.'[20] To the man behind the *nom de plume* (pen name), God's gracious work progressively re-

---

16. *Sermons I*, vol. 1 of The Bicentennial Edition of the Works of John Wesley, ed. Albert C. Outler (Nashville, TN, 1984), 121

17. *Sermons II*, vol. 2 of The Bicentennial Edition of the Works of John Wesley, ed. Albert C. Outler (Nashville, TN, 1985), 156.

18. See *Journals and Diaries II*, vol. 19 of The Bicentennial Edition of the Works of John Wesley, ed. W. Reginald Ward and Richard P. Heitzenrater (Nashville, TN, 1990), 19. '[Upon] the whole, although I have not yet that joy in the Holy Ghost, nor that love of God shed abroad in my heart, nor the full assurance of faith, nor the (proper) witness of the Spirit with my spirit that I am a child of God…I nevertheless trust that I have a measure of faith and am "accepted in the Beloved"'.

19. See 'Justification by Faith' (1746) in *Sermons I*, 193.

20. *Letters II*, 140.

stored humanity. The Spirit's supernatural way of operation was categorically insensible. Functioning beyond our capacity for intellection, the inspiration of God in Spirit was imperceptible.

Wesley contended that insofar as righteousness, peace, and joy were sensible, so too was the inspiration of the Holy Spirit. When a person perceived these, he or she had encountered the operative presence of the Spirit of God. However, Smith insisted that these constituted the natural effects of the Spirit's inspiration, and not the operation itself. Thus, Smith made the following distinction: '"Natural", "ordinary", and "common", when spoken of God's actions, I take to be…synonymous terms. "Supernatural", "miraculous", and "uncommon" are likewise synonyms.'[21] This being the case, he took Wesley to task on the issue: 'The question to be debated, then, [is] not whether the *fruits* of inspiration are… perceptible, but whether *the work* of inspiration itself be so; whether the work of God's Spirit in us be as easily distinguishable from the workings of our own spirit as light is from darkness.'[22] Smith remained convinced that his opponent had shifted the issue of perceptible inspiration, by focusing instead on its sensible or 'natural' effects (*viz.,* the fruits of righteousness, peace, joy, and love).

Sensing the strength of his opponent's argument, Wesley made a further distinction of his own: 'You objected that I held perceptible inspiration. I answered, I do; but observe in what sense (otherwise I must recall my concession). I hold, God *inspires* every Christian with peace and joy and love, which are all *perceptible*.'[23] By the term 'inspiration', Wesley here meant the fruits of peace, joy, and love (holiness) as affected in a believer by the Spirit of God. This, however, did not include the metaphysical operations of God. Wesley further expounded this distinction with the following remarks: '[by] the "operations" of the Spirit I do not mean the manner in which he operates, but the graces which he operates in a Christian.'[24] As he explained it, the inner-dynamics of the Spirit's operation were imperceptible, since they transcended the limits of human finitude. Still, while its manner was ineffable, the grace wrought by the Spirit was as clearly perceptible as light and

21. *Letters II,* 168.
22. *Letters II,* 188.
23. *Letters II,* 202.
24. *Letters II,* 203.

darkness. Wesley was scarcely concerned with speculation upon the Spirit
of God *ad intra* (or within the Godhead). This being the case, his theology
of perceptible inspiration was a meditation on the Holy Spirit's activities in
the economy of salvation; and to the extent that peace, joy, and love spring-
ing from faith-filled assurance was directly sensible, so too were the inspiring
activities of God's Divine Spirit.

However, while Wesley defined perceptible inspiration in terms of
its physically perceptible fruits, he was even more convinced that believers
could spiritually sense the direct witness of the Holy Spirit. Indeed, said Wesley, 'over and above those other graces which the Holy Spirit inspires into or
operates in a Christian, and over and above his imperceptible influences, I
do intend all mankind should understand me to assert' that 'every Christian
believer hath a perceptible testimony of the Spirit that he is a child of God.'[25]
Wesley believed that the testimony of the Spirit, which offered assurance to
sons and daughters of God, was a gift beheld through direct spiritual perception. More than the physical evidence of outward holiness, perceptible inspiration was also a supernatural gift from God, through which believers were
brought to consciousness of the Holy Spirit's operation within the economy
of salvation.

Throughout their correspondence, perceptible inspiration was central to Wesley's theology. In his view, grace, faith, and spiritual consciousness
needed always to germinate the fruits of inward and outward holiness. To
him, this fundamental truth rested at the core of the human/Spirit relationship, and comprised the way of the Spirit within the economy of salvation.
Perceptible inspiration reflected the self-disclosing nature of the Holy Spirit
who breathed filial confidence, peace, joy, and love into the souls of faithful
believers.

What is interesting, however, is that Wesley (according to my rsearch
so far) never again uses the expression perceptible inspiration in his writings.
Although he espoused it throughout his correspondence with Smith—arguing its importance as the condition of salvation—the exact phrase does not
appear in the rest of his entire body of work. Why might this be? Was it actually as important as Wesley maintained, or had he exaggerated it, in order
to 'chop logic' with a worthy opponent? In this author's opinion, it was the

---

25. *Letters II*, 232.

former. Although Wesley never used the expression again, the underlying significance of perceptible inspiration as *via Spiritus* was the essence of his theology of God's Holy Spirit, and a rondo repeated throughout the whole of his works. Theological expressions like 'true religion', 'heart religion', 'spiritual consciousness', 'spiritual respiration', and 'spiritual birth' (which Wesley did repeat) all embodied his theology of grace, faith, the witness of the Spirit and love. These four were fundamental to his thinking—the 'substance' of what every Methodist ought to preach. Therefore, although the term may never have been uttered again by Wesley, the key expressions of grace, faith, the witness of the Spirit, and the fruits of the Spirit (or what I call *via Spiritus*) were. And their collective significance as participation in the life of God remained a lifelong fixture of his theology and mission.

The Epistemological Question

Smith's letters had raised another important question. How can a person know whether he or she has actually perceived the inspiration of the Holy Spirit, or been deluded by an overactive imagination? To use his words: 'In short, as the enthusiast[26] seems as confident of his inspiration as one really inspired is of his, a third person hath a right to call for other proof than confident assertion.'[27] In other words, Smith desired proof of perceptible inspiration, proof that the experiences of 'inspirants' were authentic. Forcing Wesley on the issue, he asked: 'in what sense is that attestation [from the Holy Spirit] infallible, and plainly discernible from fancy, which they who *have not* may fancy they have, and they who *really have* may fancy they have it not?'[28] In other words, how could direct knowledge of the witness of the Holy Spirit be infallibly demonstrated?

Wesley's response to this question is all but bewildering for a man whose theological method is supposedly shaped by the authority of reason.[29]

---

26. For Wesley and his contemporaries, the term 'enthusiast' denoted any person falsely laying claim to inspiration; 'enthusiasm' was tantamount to religious fanaticism.

27. *Letters II*, 241.

28. *Letters II*, 167-168. Italics mine.

29. Much work has been done on Wesley's implicit method in theology and the authoritative role of reason within it. See Donald Thorsen, *The Wesleyan Quadrilateral: Scripture, Tradition, Reason, and Experience as a Model of Evangelical Theology* (Nappanee, IN,

How could a believer know that he or she had rightly perceived inspiration; or to use Smith's question, '[in] what sense is that attestation of the Spirit *infallible*?'[30] To this Wesley gave the following, seemingly sub-rational reply:

> In no sense at all. And yet, though I allow that some may fancy they have it when in truth they have it not, I cannot allow that any fancy they have it not at the time when they really have. I know no instance of this. When they have this faith they cannot possibly doubt of their having it, although 'tis very possible, when they have it not, they may doubt whether ever they had it or no.[31]

Wesley believed that 'false inspiration' was possible. However, in the same breath, he staunchly maintained that none who *actually* perceived the Spirit's inspiration could think otherwise. In the moment when believers were imbued the witness or testimony, they could not doubt its authenticity. Believers simply 'felt' or knew it. Though the fruits of the Spirit served as objective criteria for gauging the authenticity of one's inspiration, the only subjective criterion was personal participation.

To be sure, however, Wesley's definition of 'feeling' was not synonymous with that of emotion. Rather, it denoted a broader knowledge-based sensitivity. According to Theodore Runyon, feeling 'was [Wesley's] designation for the sensations mediated by the spiritual senses to the "heart," the center of the psychosomatic unity of the person.' In other words, it was an inward consciousness of 'the heart but to the reason as well.'[32] Spiritual feeling, which occurred during inspiration, was participation in God's divine reality, and by its nature, transcendent of demonstrable or empirical proof.

Was Wesley being irrational, did he tend toward enthusiasm as Smith maintained, or were the two clergymen simply arguing using disparate

---

1990) and Rebekah Miles, 'The Instrumental Role of Reason', in *Wesley and the Quadrilateral: Renewing the Conversation* (Nashville, TN, 1997), 77-106.

30. *Letters II*, 177. Though uncomfortable with the term, 'infallible', Wesley allowed it for the sake of dialectic. '"Infallible testimony" was *your* word, not *mine*. I never use it. I do not like it. But I did not object to *your* using that phrase, because I would not fight about words.'

31. *Letters II*, 178.

32. Runyon, *The New Creation*, 152.

conceptions of knowledge? Wesley, unlike his adversary, was disinterested in epistemology. Stephen Long argues that:

> [Wesley] did not seem burdened by the need to come up with some theory that would relate our mind to the world. Instead, he presents us with a "spiritual sensorium" that uncritically mixes an Augustinian theory of illumination (mediated through Cambridge Platonism) with the sensibility of knowledge plundered from Locke, which Wesley assumed did not conflict with Aristotle...[33]

According to Stephen Long, Wesley's theology of knowledge 'is something much more like Aquinas's work than anything that follows from the significant philosophical changes that occurred in the eighteenth century'.[34] In other words, Wesley's epistemic theology was non-epistemological;[35] it was based on a metaphysic of participation, or participatory knowledge, which extended from the Neoplatonic tradition in St Augustine up through Cambridge Platonism, where Wesley most likely encountered it.

Spiritual knowledge for Wesley was not propositional or conceptual, but relational. Our 'capability for God',[36] as Wesley expressed it, was not built for the formation of ideas, but for intimacy. We do not use our spiritual senses to construct divine ideas *per se* (as the empiricist view would hold), but to experience the 'life of God in the human soul'.[37] Thus, while Wesley's

---

33. Long, *John Wesley's Moral Theology*, 13.

34. Long, *John Wesley's Moral Theology*, 13.

35. The author of this essay distinguishes between the terms, 'epistemology' and 'epistemic theology'. The former conceives of reason as a secular tool of apprehension; the latter presupposes that all knowledge is grounded in God's self-revelation and the *telos* (or purpose) of union with the Spirit. John Wesley was wholeheartedly convinced of the importance of knowledge, but for theological reasons—true knowledge was participation in God's divine life.

36. See 'The Deceitfulness of the Human Heart' in *Sermons IV*, vol. 4 of The Bicentennial Edition of the Works of John Wesley, ed. Albert C. Outler (Nashville, TN, 1987), 153.

37. 'Dost thou know what religion is?' '[It] is a participation of the divine nature, the life of God in the soul of man'. See Charles Wesley's sermon, 'Awake, Thou That Sleepest' (1742), in *Sermons I*, 150. John Wesley included his brother's homily in his 1746 publication of *Sermons on Several Occasions*. The phrase 'life of God in the human soul', how-

use of 'spiritual perception' language was couched in the idiom of empiricism, his underlying sympathies were more in line with a metaphysic of participation, wherein God illuminated the human soul and inspired the heart with a 'divine conviction of things unseen'.[38] In Wesley's theology, divine knowledge was received and experienced as the gift of the Holy Spirit. This being the case, his oft-employed metaphor of spiritual sensation was simply that—a figurative expression, aimed to make sense of humanity's participation in the life of God, which took shape in the parlance of sense perception. As Wesley put it, we are 'figuratively said to *see* [by] the light of faith'.[39] And in his 1790 sermon 'On Living Without God', regarding spiritual sensation, he claimed: 'it may easily be observed that the substance of all these figurative expressions is comprised in that one word "faith", taken in its widest sense; being enjoyed, more or less, by everyone that believes in the name of the Son of God.'[40] In Wesley's theology, spiritual sensation was a metaphor for faith, which was our faculty for participatory knowledge of the divine.

Unfortunately, some have pushed this metaphor to the extreme. Rex Matthews, whose 1986 doctoral dissertation represents one of the most thorough treatments of Wesley and epistemology to date, has described Wesley's epistemic theology in terms of 'transcendental empiricism': '"empiricism" because of his insistence that there are no innate ideas of any sort and that everything in the mind must first come via the senses;' and '"transcendental" because of his argument for the existence of the "spiritual senses" of faith, which are the avenues to perception of spiritual reality.'[41] However, such a

---

ever, comes from Henry Scougal's same titled work, *The Life of God in the Soul of Man, or the Nature and Excellency of the Christian Religion, with the Method of Obtaining the Happiness it Proposes*, which John Wesley abridged and published in 1746.

38. See 'On Faith' (1791), in *Sermons IV*, 188. According to Wesley, 'faith is, in one sense of the word, a divine conviction of God and of the things of God; in another (nearly related to, yet not altogether the same) it is a divine conviction of the invisible and eternal world.'

39. *The Appeals*, 171.

40. *Sermons IV*, 173.

41. Matthews, '"Religion and Reason Joined"', 309. George Croft Cell, *The Rediscovery of John Wesley* (New York, 1935), 93. See also Mitsuo Shimizu, 'Epistemology in the Thought of John Wesley' Ph.D. Diss. (Drew University, 1980), 170-172. Both Matthews and Shimizu mistake the 'spiritual senses' for a literal ontological faculty endued in born again Christians.

phrase does little more than to literalize the metaphor of 'spiritual sensation'. Though Matthews rightly demonstrates that Wesley's theology of spiritual knowledge was more supernatural than contemporaries like 'John Smith' allowed, the phrase 'transcendental empiricism' does not take seriously the major premise of all strains of empiricism—namely, that the senses relate to the physical world, and can thus only function when confronted by physical matter.

Wesley's epistemic theology, upon closer inspection, seems to be less commensurate with empiricism, and more continuous with the knowledge of direct spiritual participation. This is evinced by the mounted theological tension between he and John Smith in their written exchange. Smith flatly stated that he would 'believe nothing without proofs.'[42] Thomas Oden labelled this approach 'Rationalistic Skepticism', explaining that its proponents believed 'even if God has saved humanity, no finite beholder could dependably perceive it, since such claims are intrinsically…unknowable.'[43] Since Wesley could provide nothing demonstrable to verify the believer's subjective experience of the direct witness of the Spirit, the two men were unable to reach common ground on the issue of perceptible inspiration.

Conclusion

When critically approached, the 'John Smith' correspondence demonstrates that Wesley's theology of knowledge owes less to early-modern empiricism than many have supposed. Stephen Long makes the convincing argument that Wesley's theology of 'spiritual sensation', though expressed in the language of sense perception, was at heart a knowledge of intimacy, or participation. In this respect, his epistemic theology clashed with his opponent's epistemology, which led Wesley and Smith ultimately to disagree on the issue.

Furthermore, the correspondence is also significant in terms of understanding John Wesley's pneumatology. Throughout their exchange, Wesley continually stressed the theological importance of perceptible in-

---

42. *Letters II*, 261.

43. Thomas C. Oden, *John Wesley's Scriptural Christianity: A Plain Exposition of His Teaching on Christian Doctrine* (Grand Rapids, MI, 1994), 229.

spiration. More than a religious epistemology, perceptible inspiration was the essence of John Wesley's economic pneumatology. It was his theology of *via Spiritus*, or way of the Spirit, within the sphere of human experience and salvation. To Wesley, this 'way' of the Spirit commenced with the gift of grace, by which believers were enabled to respond with faith. Upon receiving faith, men and women perceived the witness of the Spirit and produced the fruits of love and holiness in their lives. Wesley continually stressed the importance of these soteriological features throughout his writings. Thus, it is clear that the *via Spiritus* of perceptible inspiration was essential to his pneumatology, and is a suitable model for further appraisal of his theology of the Holy Spirit.

Finally, what practical implication does Wesley's theology of perceptible inspiration offer contemporary scholars? As shown above, Wesley embraced the notion that the Holy Spirit provided an inward, cognizable testimony of divine fellowship to human beings. In his view, such was an indication of God's communicative nature; it meant that the Father of all spirits, who drew near to men and women of faith, was intimately knowable. When viewed through this lens, the picture that emerges of Wesley's practical theology becomes clear: since inspiration is perceptible, the nature of the Holy Spirit is self-revelatory. God seeks self-disclosure. In order to be faithful to its namesake, Wesley studies (especially those in theology) must always be framed by his commitment to the relational nature of God's Holy Spirit.

JOHN WESLEY'S
COVENANTAL AND DISPENSATIONAL VIEW OF
SALAVTION HISTORY

J. Russell Frazier

John Wesley, reflecting the spirit of the Enlightenment, had a deep appreciation of the importance of history.[1] He, in fact, edited and published a number
of histories notably Henry Brooke's *The History of Henry Earl of Moreland,*[2] *A
Concise History of England*[3] and *A Concise Ecclesiastical History, from the Birth
of Christ, to the Beginning of the Present Century.*[4] Glenn Burt Hosman, in his
dissertation entitled 'The Problem of Church and State in the Thought of
John Wesley as Reflecting His Understanding of Providence and His View
of History', explains that one of the reasons Wesley wanted to prepare books
about history for the Methodists was because he believed that well-written
history was instructive. Hosman writes,

---

1. Ken MacMillan, 'John Wesley and the Enlightened Historians', *Methodist History* 38, 3 (January 2000), 125.

2. Henry Brooke, *The History of Henry, Earl of Moreland*, ed. John Wesley (London,
1781).

3. John Wesley, *A Concise History of England, from the Earliest Times, to the Death of George II*, 4
vols. (London, 1776).

4. John Wesley, *A Concise Ecclesiastical History: From the Birth of Christ to the Beginning of the
Present Century*, 4 vols. (London, 1781).

In almost romantic language, Wesley has described his view of history. History, when most fully understood, reveals God's Truth. History is instructive of the doctrines of religion, and it inspires one toward gratitude to God and goodness to man. In other words, History is the record of the dialogic relationships of God and man, and man and neighbour, if indeed they can be so dichotomized.[5]

For Wesley, a study of history provided an explanation of the providence of God within history displaying divine wisdom in God's interactions with human beings. Hosman's starting point is the political writings of Wesley, and while he addressed the idea of providence and Wesley's view of history, his conclusions are limited by the scope of his work.

A number of other writers have addressed Wesley's view of history. In 'Wesley's Views on the Uses of History', Joseph Seaborn examines Wesley's purpose in writing history and reveals that Wesley wrote history to 'aid them [Methodists] in holy living in the present and ultimately lead them to a future in heaven'.[6] Ted Campbell analyses Wesley's refutation of Conyers Middleton's thesis that miracles, defined as the intervention of God in history, occurred only in apostolic times.[7] Ken MacMillan, in 'John Wesley and the Enlightened Historians', concluded '...Wesley attempted to reconcile his belief in providential history with science and reason, believing that when properly understood, and its limitations recognized, empiricism could show what God has wrought in history'.[8] In 'Methodism in a Philosophy of History', William Cannon analyzed what he called Wesley's 'anatomy of history' based upon the following outline: 'creation, the fall, the universality of evil, the incarnation of God in Jesus Christ, the universal scope of the atonement,

---

5. Glenn Burt Hosman, 'The Problem of Church and State in the Thought of John Wesley as Reflecting His Understanding of Providence and His View of History' (Ph.D. diss., Drew University, 1970), 188. See John Wesley, *Explanatory Notes upon the New Testament* (London, 1950; Alec. R. Allenson Inc., 1966), on Matthew 24:14, where Wesley comments that Josephus's *History of the Jewish War* is the best commentary on the chapter.

6. Joseph W. Seaborn, 'Wesley's Views on the Uses of History', *Wesleyan Theological Journal* 21, 1 and 2 (Spring-Fall 1986), 130.

7. Ted A. Campbell, 'John Wesley and Conyers Middleton on Divine Intervention in History', *Church History* 55, 1 (March 1986), 39.

8. MacMillan, 131.

the claim on and application of its benefits....'[9] Cannon's article falls short because he fails to examine the structure of salvation history which Wesley explicitly employs: covenants and dispensations. In fact, none of these articles has examined the structure of salvation history which Wesley posited. MacMillan addresses Wesley's view of history as a polemic against deism, but none of these writers discusses Wesley's view of history in light of the Wesley's polemic against Calvinism. This essay will examine Wesley's view of salvation history as reflected in his treatment of the doctrine of the providence of God and his theology of covenants and dispensations giving special attention to the implications for Wesley's polemic against Calvinism.

The Doctrine of Divine Providence

In his preface to *A Concise History of England* (1776), Wesley notes several concerns with previous histories of England: firstly, the works are not concise enough for the average reader; secondly, the authors are not impartial and write from their own particular political point of view; thirdly, many historians wrote from an atheistic or deistic perspective. Wesley elaborates the last point

> ...for there is nothing about God in them. Who would gather from these accounts, who would have the least suspicion, that it is God who governs the world? That his kingdom ruleth over all, in Heaven above, and in earth beneath? That he alone changeth the times and the seasons, removeth kings and setteth up kings, and disposes all things by his almighty power, according to the counsels of his own will? Nay, rather from the whole tenor of their discourse one would suppose, that God was quite out of the question....[10]

God, for Wesley, is active and intricately involved within the history of the world and every aspect of creation. God's concern and providential care of creation demonstrates divine love for all creation.

---

9. William R. Cannon, 'Methodism in a Philosophy of History', *Methodist History* 12 (July 1974), 34.

10. Wesley, *A Concise History of England*, v-iv.

Wesley links explicitly the doctrine of God as creator and the doctrine of the love of God. In his letter dated 4 January 1749 to Dr Conyers Middleton, Wesley responds to the question, 'Who is a Christian indeed?' and compares the Christian's love to the love of God whose love is impartial in that it extends to all of creation.[11] The Christian is content knowing that there is an 'intelligent Cause and Lord of all' and that the Creator disseminates goodness to the benefit of all creatures.[12] Christians take comfort not only in the thought of the transcendent God who rules over all things with a general providential care for all creation, but also in the thought that God's care extends to every person: in Wesley's words, '...so presiding over every single person as if he were the whole universe...'[13] Kenneth Collins points out that Wesley stressed the doctrine of the particular providence of God, which was significant in his thought, against those who held only to a general providence of God.[14] God's general and particular providential care over creation is rooted in God's essential nature.

The Doctrine of the Heathen

As was noted above, the doctrine of divine providence is rooted in the doctrine of the love of God. Wesley emphasized the love of God and the concomitant doctrine of the universal extent of the atonement. In disavowing the doctrine of particular predestination,[15] it became impingent upon him to demonstrate the atonement's extent not only for all persons who were alive in his day but for all human beings who had ever lived since the beginning of time. Was the atonement effective only for those who lived subsequent to the death of Christ? Is God the God of the heathen as well as the God of Christians? Was the atonement efficacious for Abraham, for example, who was the father of faith, but who did not know of the ministry and atoning work

---

11. John Wesley, *The Letters of the Rev. John Wesley*, ed. John Telford, 8 vols. (London, 1931), 2:377.

12. Wesley, *Letters*, 2:379.

13. Wesley, *Letters*, 2:379.

14. Kenneth J. Collins, *The Theology of John Wesley: Holy Love and the Shape of Grace* (Nashville, TN, 2007), 40-42. The primary target of these polemical attacks was the deists.

15. Particular predestination is the doctrine that God determined from all eternity the final salvation of every individual.

of Christ? Wesley recognized the implications of the doctrine of universal atonement and developed what, in eighteenth-century language, might be called a 'doctrine of the heathen'.

One of Wesley's most explicit elaborations of his view of history appears in the sermon entitled, 'On Divine Providence' (1786). In the introduction of this sermon, he cites the testimony of an Indian chief, Paustoobee, who acknowledged an awareness of the protective care of God.[16] Despite the conviction that heathens have an awareness of God, Wesley argued that their knowledge of God's providential dealings with the world were very limited and imperfect. God alone can give 'a consistent, perfect account...of his manner of governing the world'.[17]

One Unbroken Chain

For Wesley, Scripture reveals this 'consistent, perfect account' of God's governance of the world; Wesley asserts, '...Scripture is *the history of God*'.[18] The inspired writers constantly remembered that the story of the human race is ultimately God's story, and they 'preserve one unbroken, connected chain, from beginning to end.'[19]

How could Wesley hold that the Scriptures preserve 'one unbroken, connected chain' given the disparity of the biblical record which particularly seems apparent between the Old and New Testaments? Like the Caroline Divines, Wesley held to a teleological view of salvation history which led from the creation, to the Fall, to the full restoration at the *eschaton*.[20] Ultimately, history finds its apex in Christ. History and providence merge into the person and life of Jesus Christ.[21] For Wesley, Christ gives 'meaning and content to all History, past, present, and future. If God is not in historical events then History, becomes the grotesque cataloguing of unimportant trivia. It is

16. John Wesley, *Sermons II, 34-70*, vol. 2 of The Bicentennial Edition of the Works of John Wesley, ed. Albert C. Outler (Nashville, TN, 1985), 535. Hereafter: Wesley, *BE Works*.

17. Wesley, *BE Works*, 2:536.

18. John Wesley, *A Concise History of England*, 536, emphasis in the original.

19. John Wesley, *A Concise History of England*, 536.

20. Cary Balzer, 'John Wesley's Developing Soteriology and the Influence of the Caroline Divines', (Ph. D. thesis, University of Manchester (Nazarene Theological College), 2005), 144.

21. Hosman, 176.

the God with us, Immanuel, which elevates mundane human and cosmic encounter into History with eternal significance.'[22] God revealed himself fully in Christ. Salvation history demonstrates the activity of the Holy Spirit in bringing about the full restoration of humanity to the image of God as revealed in Christ. Sanctification is the process of the restoration in the image of God; perfection of believers is the *telos* of God's redemptive activity.

Providence of Degrees

Because God is love, creator of all things, and omniscient, God cares deeply for human beings and knows them intimately. According to Wesley, God is an administrator or manager of grace who bestows grace in its appropriate measures based upon his knowledge of the human condition. Grace is dispensed according to the measure of humanity's ability to receive it. This accounts, to some degree, for the disparity between the Old and New Testaments and the inequality between the different degrees of administration of divine grace. Wesley stated '...it has been remarked by a pious author that there is (as he expresses it) a threefold circle of divine providence over and above that which presides over the whole world'.[23] Wesley referred to these three concentric circles in another later sermon entitled, 'Spiritual Worship' (1780).[24] The writer to whom Wesley refers is Thomas Crane, author of *Isagoge ad Dei Providentiam, Or a Prospect of Divine Providence* (1672) which Wesley extracted for his *Christian Library* (1749-1755). In 'Observation XIII', entitled 'Providence hath its different Courts, in which the Sons of Men have their different Stations', Crane wrote of three concentric circles of the providence of God:

> 1. There is the outermost circle of common providence: here all men may be placed. "The Lord madeth his sun to shine on the evil and the good, and sendeth rain on the just and on the unjust." (Matt. v.45) "Nevertheless, he left not himself without a witness, in that he

22. Hosman, 176.

23. Wesley, *BE Works*, 2:541-542, 'On Divine Providence', (1786).

24. John Wesley, *Sermons III, 71-114*, vol. 3 of The Bicentennial Edition of the Works of John Wesley, ed. Albert C. Outler (Nashville, TN, 1986), 94.

did good, and gave us rain from heaven, and fruitful seasons, filling our hearts with food and gladness." (Acts xiv.17.)

2. There is an intermediate circle of special providence, which respects members of the visible Church. Unto the Jews "were committed the oracles of God:" they are called the children of the kingdom, "inasmuch as God" honoured them with his worship and ordinances.

3. There is the inmost circle of peculiar providence. In this circle are the children of God. The former of larger circumference than this latter; "for many are called, but few are chosen." (Matt. xxii. 14.) The Apostle Paul doth describe this by a house in which are vessels of divers sorts, not only vessels of gold and silver, but also of wood and of earth; some to honour, and some to comparative dishonour.[25]

In Wesley's summary of Crane's 'courts' or concentric circles of providence which he addressed in his sermon 'On Divine Providence' (1786), Wesley emphasized that the providential care of God extends to all creatures: '... Is he the God of the Christians, and not of the Mahometans and heathens also? Yea, doubtless of the Mahometans and heathens also. His love is not confined...'[26] While the concentric circles depict God's providential care for all human beings, they also demonstrate the various degrees of God's care; the smallest circle includes all Christians who are the recipients of God's most intimate care. Wesley pointed out that such particularities should not be surprising; God cares more for human beings than for animals.[27] Furthermore, God can suspend the laws of nature to accomplish a miracle for an individual or a group of people as at the Red Sea for the nation of Israel.[28]

The doctrine of divine providence provides a foundation for Wesley's view of history. The love of God pervades all of creation and history.

---

25. [Thomas Crane], 'A Prospect of Divine Providence', *A Christian Library: Consisting of Extracts from and Abridgments of the Choicest Pieces of Practical Divinity Which Have Been Written in the English Tongue*, ed. John Wesley, vol. 22 of 30 vols. (London, 1825), 431-432.

26. Wesley, *BE Works*, 2:542.

27. Wesley, *BE Works*, 2:544.

28. Wesley, *BE Works*, 2:546.

This doctrine of the all pervasive love of God was the starting point for Wesley's polemic against the Calvinistic doctrine of particular predestination. Wesley could not reconcile the doctrine of particular predestination with his understanding of God. It was too discriminatory and arbitrary, and the God of Calvinism was too capricious.

The Structure of Wesley's View of History

Wesley's doctrine of divine providence provides a foundation for his view of history that remained relatively intact throughout his life. Despite the fact that the essential foundation for Wesley's view of history never underwent any substantial change, it has been asserted that the structure of his concept of history did undergo change. [29] As will become evident, Wesley employed and emphasized covenant theology in his early sermons. He evidenced later a greater penchant for employing the term 'dispensation' in his discussions of salvation history.

The structure of Wesley's view of salvation history comes to expression within his concept of covenants and dispensations. As the love of God was foundational for the doctrine of divine providence and Wesley's view of history, the love of God was also foundational for the structure of salvation history. Wesley stated in his notes on Ephesians 3:9, 'This [love] is the foundation for all his dispensations.'[30]

Covenant Theology in Wesley's Early Sermons and Writings

Wesley's sermon, 'The Righteousness of Faith' (1746), gives the fullest description of his covenant theology.[31] At the outset of the sermon, the Jewish

---

29. John Allan Knight, 'John William Fletcher and the Early Methodist Tradition' (Ph.D. diss., Vanderbilt University, 1966), 20.

30. John Wesley, *Explanatory Notes upon the New Testament* (London, 1950; Alec. R. Allenson Inc., 1966), Eph. 3.9 (in loco). Hereafter, references to the *Notes* will be indicated in the text by citing the reference to the passage of scripture.

31. See also John Wesley, *The Works of John Wesley, Complete and Unabridged.* 14 vols., (London, 1872; Baker Book House, 1991), 9:333, 403-404, 418. See Collins, *The Theology of John Wesley,* 65. Wesley addressed the issue in Question 24 of the Minutes of 1746. See the discussion in Harald Lindström, *Wesley and Sanctification: A Study in the Doctrine of Salvation* (Nashville, TN, n.d.), 208-209.

dispensation is clearly linked to the covenant of grace. Revealing his Puritan leanings, Wesley taught that the covenant of works which was established with supralapsarian Adam[32] as the federal head of the human race requiring perfect obedience of him and his posterity was fulfilled and abolished by the work of Christ. In Wesley's thought, the impossibility of attaining justification under the terms of this covenant is forcefully underscored. Wesley appealed to the doctrine of the covenant of works to emphasize the impossibility of good works as a means of entry into the Christian life. Although established by God with infralapsarian Adam,[33] the covenant of grace was fulfilled by the atoning work of Christ and requires faith; God "'imputes his [the believer's] faith to him for righteousness'."[34] The righteousness of the law may be summarized by the words 'Do this and live'; whereas the righteousness of faith may best be summarized by the words 'Believe and live'.[35] Supralapsarian Adam was the only human being who was under the covenant of works; all other human beings are under the covenant of grace. At this point, Wesley's emphasis on the initiative of divine grace is evident in the way that he describes the place of good works within the Christian life: 'I rejoice because I both see and feel, through the inspiration of God's Holy Spirit, that all my works are wrought in him, yea, and that it is he who worketh all my works in me'.[36]

Notably, Wesley does not give space in this sermon to the doctrine of the covenant of redemption. In a letter to his brother, Charles, on 2 June 1775, he recognized the centrality of the doctrine to the Calvinist system: 'I purpose writing to Mr. Fletcher shortly. I do not remember that he has touched the corner-stone of their hypothesis, "the covenant of redemption". One would not wish to be easy without it. Just here we must stop reasoning, or turn Calvinists. This is the very strength of their cause'.[37] In his preface to *A Treatise on Justification*, Wesley rebutted James Hervey's doctrine of the covenant of redemption. Wesley denied any biblical foundation or historic-

---

32. 'Supralapsarian' means prior to the Fall.

33. 'Infralapsarian' indicates after the Fall.

34. John Wesley, *Sermons I, 1-33*, vol. 1 of The Bicentennial Edition of the Works of John Wesley, ed. Albert C. Outler (Nashville, TN, 1984), 207.

35. Wesley, *BE Works*, 1:204.

36. Wesley, *BE Works*, 1:310, 'The Witness of Our Own Spirit,' (1746).

37. Wesley, *Works*, 12:143.

ity to the doctrine: "'Tis sure, He did every Thing necessary: But how does it appear, that he undertook this, before the Foundation of the World, and that by a positive Covenant between Him and the Father".[38] Again, 'They [the texts cited by Hervey] do by no means prove, That there ever was any such Covenant made between the Father and the Son'.[39] Thus, one of the reasons that Wesley rejected the covenant of redemption was because it was ahistorical.

While Wesley used covenantal language in his preface, he endeavoured to avoid the errors of the Calvinistic doctrine of the covenants. Wesley countered Hervey's argument that the covenant of grace had changed the locus of obedience from man to Christ by asserting that this is an unscriptural way of speaking. When Hervey argues that the covenant of grace was not made with Adam and his posterity but with Christ, Wesley argues that the words were not spoken *to* Christ but *of* him and give 'no intimation of any such covenant...'[40] Wesley argues that Christ did not fulfil the conditions of the covenant of grace; human beings by grace can fulfil the conditions of the covenant which are, in part, repentance and faith. 'What Christ has done is the foundation, not the condition of our justification....Wesley...described the new covenant made possible by Christ's sacrificial death and making possible human participation in the covenant through faith'.[41] To assert otherwise is to fall into the trap of antinomianism. Wesley's evident concern with the Calvinist doctrine of the covenants is the theoretical antinomianism inherent therein.

In his sermon, 'The Righteousness of Faith', Wesley made a distinction between two dispensations, the Mosaic or Jewish dispensation and the gospel dispensation, both of which can be classified under the covenant of grace. Wesley restricts Christ's abolishment of the law to the ritual law of the Mosaic dispensation. When Wesley describes the state of the 'natural man' who is under the law, he links it closely to the Jewish dispensation, but his intention is to delineate the existential response of human beings to the law

---

38.   John Wesley, *A Treatise on Justification: Extracted from Mr. John Goodwin With a Preface, Wherein All That is Material, in Letters Just Published, Under the Name of the Rev. Mr. Hervey, is Answered.* (Bristol, 1765), 15.

39.   Robert C. Monk, *John Wesley: His Puritan Heritage* (Nashville, TN, 1966), 16.

40.   Wesley, *A Treatise on Justification*, 16.

41.   Balzer, 233.

rather than to describe the nature of the law or to differentiate it from the gospel.[42] Christ was 'made under the law' (Gal 4:4) or the Jewish dispensation which included the moral and ceremonial law in order to redeem the Jews from that dispensation. However, Wesley further catalogued the covenants 'in maintaining a progressively fuller and clearer revelation of this covenant from Adam through Abraham, Moses, David and the prophets'.[43] Robert Monk points out that for Wesley the covenants which God made with the aforementioned persons were valid covenants of grace due to the fact that they were based upon faith; however, they were incomplete and point toward the final covenant which was accomplished by Christ. Thus, a degree of progression is evident in the history of revelation in Wesley's thought.[44]

In his sermon, 'Christian Perfection' (1741),[45] Wesley affirms that the dispensation of John the Baptist was greater than the previous dispensations, and the present Christian dispensation supersedes that of John.

> The plain consequence is, the least of these who have now Christ for their King is greater than he. Not "a greater prophet" (as some have interpreted the word), for this is palpably false in fact, but greater in the grace of God and the knowledge of our Lord Jesus Christ. Therefore we cannot measure the privileges of real Christians by those formerly given to the Jews. "Their ministration" (or dispensation) we allow "was glorious"; but ours "exceeds in glory" so that whosoever would bring down the Christian dispensation to the Jewish standard, whosoever gleans up the examples of weakness recorded in the law and the prophets, and thence infers that they who have "put on Christ" are endued with no greater strength, doth "greatly err, neither knowing the Scriptures nor the power of God".[46]

42. Wesley, *BE Works*, 1:250.

43. Monk, 99.

44. Lawrence Wood insists that Wesley employs Fletcher's categories in two later sermons 'The Wisdom of God's Counsels' and 'The Mystery of Iniquity'; however, Wesley gives no evidence that he is citing Fletcher. See Laurence W. Wood, *The Meaning of Pentecost in Early Methodism: Rediscovering John Fletcher as John Wesley's Vindicator and Designated Successor*, Pietist and Wesleyan Studies 15, ed. David Bundy and J. Steven O'Malley (Oxford, 2002) 171, 176.

45. Wesley, *BE Works*, 2:98.

46. Wesley, *BE Works*, 2:108. Notably, Wesley links the dispensation of John the Baptist to the Jewish dispensation when he wants to emphasize the disparity between the Jewish and Christian

In this sermon, Wesley emphasized the discontinuity of the Mosaic and Christian dispensations. What should be evident is that Wesley is walking a tightrope of fine tuned theological distinctions: on one hand, Wesley emphasized the disparity between the inefficiency of the Mosaic dispensation and the efficiency of the Christian dispensation to achieve a moral, ethical, and spiritual transformation, and on the other hand, Wesley underlined the continuity of God's work in salvation history.

Wesley's View of History in His 'Explanatory Notes upon the New Testament'

Whereas in the earlier sermons discussed above Wesley utilized principally the term 'covenant', Wesley increasingly used the term 'dispensation' in his *Explanatory Notes upon the New Testament* (1754) to describe his view of salvation history and provided therein an implicit theology of history. Wesley contrasts the Mosaic and Christian dispensations in the *Notes*.[47]

One of the key passages in the *Notes* for an understanding of Wesley's doctrine of dispensations is found in 2 Corinthians 3 where Wesley contrasts the Mosaic and Christian dispensations.[48] The Mosaic dispensation is characterized by a veiled and limited revelation and as a 'ministration of death', and a 'ministration of condemnation'. The principle agent of the dispensation is the 'letter' of the law which results in condemnation and death. On the other hand, Wesley depicts the Christian dispensation as a revelation of Christ who is the culmination and fulfilment of the Mosaic dispensation. It is further characterized by a 'ministration of the Spirit', and a 'ministration of righteousness' and a 'liberty from servile fear, liberty from the guilt and from the power of sin liberty to behold with open face the glory of the Lord' (2 Cor. 3:17). Whereas the agent of the Mosaic dispensation was the *letter* of the law, the agent of the Christian dispensation is the *Spirit* who effects

dispensations.

47. One must remember that essential to any contrast is a basis for the contrast, i.e. some commonalities.

48. In his *Advice to Methodists, With Regard to Dress*, Wesley distinguished between the two dispensations in the following terms: '...The Jews and we are under different dispensations. The glory of the whole Mosaic dispensation was chiefly visible and external; whereas the glory of the Christian dispensation is of an invisible and spiritual nature' (Wesley, *Works*, 11:472). With this statement, Wesley dismissed the conduct of the Israelites when they adorned themselves with gold and precious stones as a good example for the Methodists.

the transformation of believers. The Christian dispensation is superior to the Mosaic dispensation precisely because the agent of the Christian dispensation is superior to the agent of the old one. The empowering Spirit of God enables an inner righteousness which is reflected in external conduct.

Other key passages in the *Notes* for understanding the doctrine of dispensations in are found in Galatians. Wesley contrasts the modes of entry into the covenant relations which characterized the Mosaic (or legal) dispensation and the Christian (or gospel) dispensation. Under the old covenant, the means of entry is circumcision, whereas under the new, the means of entry is faith (Gal. 4:6). The resulting covenantal alliances of the two dispensations differ radically: the legal dispensation leads to a bondage 'in a kind of servile state' (Gal. 3:3), and the gospel dispensation results in a relationship characterized by freedom 'from all inward and outward bondage' (Gal. 4:26). The benefits of the new covenant are made available by the Spirit who adopts those who appropriate faith (Gal. 5:4-6).

In the *Notes* on the Epistle to the Hebrews, Wesley stresses the temporal dimension of the dispensations and the abolition of the old covenant which is superseded by the superiority of the Christian dispensation. The Mosaic dispensation was abolished because it was 'weak and unprofitable, unable to make anything perfect' (Heb. 8:7); the effectiveness of the new covenant is stressed by citations of some of Wesley's favourite biblical passages: '*This is the covenant I will make after those days* – After the Mosaic dispensation is abolished. *I will put my laws in their minds* – I will open their eyes, and enlighten their understanding, to see the true, full, spiritual meaning thereof' (Heb. 9:10). The inefficiency of the old dispensation to justify or sanctify led to its abolition (Heb. 10:1).

Despite the differences between the two dispensations cited above, they share many commonalities. Wesley preserves their unity by insisting upon one common goal: Christ himself is the *teleos* of both dispensations. While the Mosaic dispensation disseminates a degree of light, the light is significantly less than the light which is disseminated in the Christian dispensation. In Deschner's words, '...the light of the Old Testament prophecy, taken in its entirety, is as a lamplight before the daylight of the New'.[49] The Mosaic dispensation finds its fulfilment in the Christian: 'The greater light swallows

---

49. John Deschner, *Wesley's Christology: An Interpretation* (Dallas, TX, 1960), 87.

up the less' (2 Cor. 3:10).[50] Wesley adds, '*So that the children of Israel could not look steadfastly to the end of that* dispensation *which is now abolished* - The end of this was Christ. The whole Mosaic dispensation tended to, and terminated in, him....' (2 Cor. 3:13). The goal of the two dispensations for humanity is the transformation and restoration of the human race in the glory of the Lord, 'His glorious love' (2 Cor. 3:18). Wesley emphasized a major difference between the two dispensations; the Mosaic dispensation is ineffective to produce transformation whereas the Christian dispensation is efficacious. This becomes evident in Wesley's description of John the Baptist's role in salvation history.

John the Baptist played a pivotal role in the unfolding of Wesley's concept of salvation history. In his comments on Matthew 11:11, Wesley affirmed that John the Baptist represents the culmination of the dispensation of the law and the prophets. John the Baptist was the greatest in the aforementioned dispensation because of his blamelessness in regard to the law, 'but he fell short of those who are perfected by the Spirit of life which is in Christ.' The experience of believers under the Christian dispensation is much greater than that of John the Baptist's because believers experience Christian regeneration and have a more perfect knowledge 'of Jesus Christ, of his redemption and kingdom, than John the Baptist had, who died before the full manifestation of the gospel.' However, not only is John the Baptist the culmination of a dispensation, Wesley depicted John as the one who 'opened a way to the most glorious dispensation of grace in the Messiah's kingdom' (Luke 1:13). The way was opened by the preaching of repentance and faith in the coming Messiah (Acts 18:25; 19:3).

In addition to the differences in the persons of Christ and John the Baptist, their ministries also differ. While Christ's and John the Baptist's messages were essentially the same focusing on ushering in the kingdom of God by repentance, the efficacy was different: John's baptism was a baptism of water prefiguring Christ's baptism 'with the Holy Ghost and with fire... which was eminently fulfilled when the Holy Ghost sat upon the disciples in the appearance of tongues, or flames of fire' (Matt. 3.6).[51] Again the same is-

---

50. Wesley in a letter 'To Dean D-' dated 1785 wrote, 'And did not He [God] use it [the Greek language] in delivering to man a far more perfect dispensation that that which He delivered in Hebrew?' (Wesley, *Letters*, 7:252).

51. The baptism of John and Christian baptism crystallize the contrast between the dispensa-

sue appears in Wesley's comparison and contrast of the 'Pentecost of Sinai in the Old Testament' and the 'Pentecost of Jerusalem in the New Testament'. These were 'the two grand manifestations of God, the legal and the evangelical; the one from the mountain, and the other from heaven; the terrible, and the merciful one' (Acts 2:1). The ministry of Christ is efficacious; Christ builds a spiritual and eternal kingdom (Acts 15:16).

The phrase 'kingdom of God' often indicates the gospel dispensation which is sometimes contrasted with the Mosaic dispensation (Matthew 3:3, 4:17, 13:24, 31) which was ineffective to accomplish pardon for sinners although it was a shadow of things to come (John 1:14). The gospel is the last dispensation of God's grace (Acts 2:17) which frees believers from the Mosaic dispensation (Rom. 8.2).

Despite his affirmation that the Mosaic dispensation has been abrogated, Wesley insisted on the validity of the moral law.[52] The moral law, he maintained, was given by 'the Son of God who delivered the law to Moses, under the character of Jehovah, and who is here spoken of as the angel of the covenant, in respect of his mediatorial office' (Acts 7:35). Thus, the moral law remains valid because the Son of God mediated it. While the law and grace were mingled together, the law, considered apart from grace, which was designed to bestow a blessing upon the human race, produces wrath due to the weakness and sinfulness of humanity. Here again, one sees a continuity and a discontinuity. Wesley insists upon the efficacy of the Christian dispensation to enable the believer to accomplish the requirements of the moral law.

Characteristics of Wesley's View of History Arising from the 'Notes'

A number of characteristics of Wesley's view of history which he emphasized in the *Notes* invite comment. The first feature is that the dispensations reveal the wisdom of God. While an understanding of the purpose of God in history is less than clear in the Mosaic dispensation, the Christian faith removes the veil which obscured an accurate understanding of Moses' writings. Faith, in the Christian dispensation, becomes a hermeneutical key which unlocks

---

tions. The baptismal formula has changed: Christian baptism was administered with the Trinitarian formula (Acts 19:3) whereas John's baptism was not.

52. Wesley, *BE Works*, 2:33-34, 'The Law Established through Faith, Discourse II' (1750).

Scripture to a fuller understanding.[53] Wesley wrote, '*The veil is taken away –* That very moment and they see, with the utmost clearness, how all the types and prophecies of the law are fully accomplished in Him' (2 Cor. 3:16).

The dispensations are a key to unlocking an understanding of the salvific activity of God in history. However, disciples may not understand at first 'the design of God's providential dispensations'; what is impingent upon them is faith 'to embrace those things' which God has not yet revealed but which will be revealed hereafter. In his comments on John 13:7, Wesley wrote, 'We do not now know perfectly any of his works, either of creation, providence, or grace. It is enough that we can love and obey now, and that we shall know hereafter'. The wisdom of God which is displayed in God's saving activity is ultimately recognized by all children of God (Luke 7:35).

A second characteristic of Wesley's view of history is that the revelation of God is accommodated to the recipients of revelation. Knowledge is revealed progressively as God accommodates divine revelation to the capacity of human beings to absorb it. Thus, knowledge is revealed in degrees: as Wesley states, '...God is wont to lead on his children by degrees, always giving them light for the present hour' (Acts 10:19-20). Yet there is a principle regarding the progress of knowledge. On Matthew 13:12, 'For whosoever hath, to him shall be given, and he shall have more abundance: but whosoever hath not, from him shall be taken away even that he hath,' Wesley points out that this verse is 'the key to all his providential dispensations.' God dispenses grace to those who are willing to receive and conceals revelation from those who are wise and prudent in the ways of the world (Matthew 11:25). In doing so, the dispensations of God demonstrate divine mercy and justice.

Thirdly, Wesley stressed that Christian ministers are stewards of the grace of God. As God dispensed grace appropriately, Christian ministers who are stewards or dispensers of God's grace are expected to do the same. According to Wesley, Paul perceives himself to be a harbinger of the gospel to the Gentiles and has 'a commission to dispense the grace of God...' (Eph. 3:2, Col. 1:25). In Wesley's introductory preface to the 'Notes on the Acts of

53. Scott J. Jones in his book, *John Wesley's Conception and Use of Scripture* (Nashville, TN, 1995), 53-58 develops the idea that Wesley used a dispensational understanding which 'allows for both continuity and change in God's relationship with humankind' (pp. 53-4).

the Apostles', he pointed out that the purpose of the book of Acts is practical because it provides Christian ministers with a method for applying truths to the various recipients of the message.

> In this book is shown the Christian doctrine, and the *method of applying it to Jews, heathens, and believers*; that is, to those who are to be converted, and those who are converted: the hindrances of it in particular men, in several kinds of men, in different ranks and nations: the propagation of the Gospel, and that grand revolution among both Jews and heathens: the victory thereof, in Spite of all opposition, from all the power, malice, and wisdom of the whole world, spreading from one chamber into temples, houses, streets, markets, fields, inns, prisons, camps, courts, chariots, ships, villages, cities, islands: to Jews, heathens, magistrates, generals, soldiers, eunuchs, captives, slaves, women, children, sailors: to Athens, and at length to Rome.[54]

Fourthly, Wesley's view of history is characterized by an emphasis on eschatology and the *teleos* of the dispensations. In Wesley's notes on 1 Corinthians 10:11, he wrote of the gospel dispensation as the last age which may include 'various periods, succeeding each other'. The present dispensation is the apex of all of history because it is the 'last administration of God's fullest grace' (Eph. 1:10). The uniqueness of this dispensation is that 'In this last great dispensation the Son alone presides' (Heb. 2:5). There is an eschatological dimension to the dispensations. In his comments on 1 John 2:18 Wesley explains that the words, 'it is the last time', mean 'The last dispensation of grace, that which is to continue to the end of time, is begun'. The dispensations include an element of 'already/not yet': the dispensation of the Messiah while it has succeeded the Mosaic dispensation 'is still in great measure to come' (Heb. 2:5).

While at times Wesley emphasized progress toward the *eschaton*, he seems in other contexts to disparage any real progress toward the goal of history. A tension between pessimism and hope is evident in his views on the state of the church. His sermon, 'On the Mystery of Iniquity' (1783),

---

54. Wesley, *Explanatory Notes*, in loco, emphasis added.

is characterized by a thread of hope which runs throughout the history of humanity. While the mystery of iniquity is evident in the periods of Noah and Abraham, evident too is the 'mystery of godliness' (1 Tim. 3:16). The pivotal event in salvation history was the day of Pentecost on which three thousand persons 'were restored to the favour and image of God...'[55] The significance of the day was due to the radical transformation of the three thousand souls: Wesley summarizes, 'Here was the dawn of the proper gospel day. Here was a proper Christian church'.[56] However, despite the transforming power so evident on the day of Pentecost, the mystery of iniquity was still manifest in the early church. Providing several examples of the shortcomings of the primitive church, Wesley traced the history of the church to point out further deficiencies of the church throughout the ages and to correct the generally positive depiction of expositors and church historians. [57] In spite of the weaknesses of the church evidenced in the lives of those who profess to be Christians, Wesley expressed his hope in the future which is tempered by his despair over the state of the church which he believed hampered the spread of the gospel.

Darren Schmidt explores this issue in his article, 'The Pattern of Revival: John Wesley's Vision of "Iniquity" and "Godliness" in Church History', in which he examines Wesley's view of the role of Methodism and the pattern of revival within church history as found in Wesley's later sermons. He addresses the question, 'How did Wesley understand the interruptions of an overarching pattern of revival in history?' Due to divine providential oversight, Wesley held that God had and would always preserve vital Christianity. Schmidt states, 'Wesley's eschatological belief demonstrates, moreover, that the pattern of "iniquity" and "godliness" was not so much a cycle as a spiral, with an upward trajectory... History was moving towards a goal, culminating in a time when holiness would prevail'.[58] Schmidt concludes by proffering

---

55. Wesley, *BE Works*, 2:454.

56. Wesley, *BE Works*, 2:455.

57. Wesley, *BE Works*, 2:456-461.

58. Darren Schmidt, 'The Pattern of Revival: John Wesley's Vision of 'Iniquity' and 'Godliness' in Church History', in Kate Cooper and Jeremy Gregory, ed. *Revival and Resurgence in Church History*, Studies in Church History 44 (Woodbridge, 2008), 150.

the idea that Wesley fused his doctrine of providence with 'a universal historical scope and language of progress', which was influenced by Enlightenment currents of thought.[59]

An Assessment of Wesley's View of History

What is evident in the discussion above is that Wesley, in the latter part of his life, developed a more explicit theology of history.[60] William Cannon affirms this view: 'There are evidences that Wesley became increasingly conscious toward the end of life of the implications of God's workings in history'.[61] John Knight affirms that the theology of history which was only implicit in Wesley's earlier work became explicit after the Calvinist controversy of the 1770s under the influence of John Fletcher's polemical response to the Calvinists.[62] How did Wesley's theology of history serve as a polemic against Calvinist soteriology? What further nuances arose in his theology of history?

The Distinction between Covenants and Dispensations in Wesley's Thought

One of the nuances which surfaced as a result of the Calvinist controversies was a distinction between covenants and dispensations in Wesley's thought. Wesley, according to John Deschner, held to both an objective and a subjective *heilsgeschichte*.[63] The objective *heilsgeschichte* was normally described by employing the terms 'covenants' or 'dispensations'. 'Covenant' is a more comprehensive term emphasizing the divine-human relationship and its requirement whereas 'dispensation' emphasizes God's administration of the plan of salvation which usually includes a greater emphasis upon the temporal quality. The covenant of grace includes both the Mosaic and the Christian dispensations. The subjective *heilsgeschichte* came to full expression in Wesley's *ordo salutis*. Both the objective and the subjective *heilsgeschichte* were

---

59. Schmidt, 151.

60. Darren Schmidt also holds that there is some evidence of progress in Wesley's thought on the subject. See Schmidt, 152.

61. Knight, 369.

62. Knight, 20.

63. Deschner, 45, 60. *Heilsgeschichte* indicates the saving activity of God in history.

essentially Christological in their orientation.[64] Deschner states that there is 'an irrepressible movement in his doctrine of Christ'.[65] Wesley's Christology demonstrates a chronological progress in the stages of Christ's history which 'admits of various degrees': glory, humiliation, and exaltation.[66]

Furthermore, 'dispensation' is often employed by Wesley in polemics against antinomianism,[67] or when he wants to address the doctrine of sanctification and to preserve the validity of the moral law while recognizing that the law no longer serves as the mode of entry into justification.[68] The notion of covenant is employed by Wesley in contexts where he wants to emphasize the doctrine of justification and to reinforce the impossibility of justification by works.[69] Covenants emphasize the continuity of salvation history, but the concept is somewhat static and does not normally allow for the variations within salvation history. Dispensations provide a platform for the continuity of the Testaments in a dynamic format, and for an emphasis on the progression of history.

Thus, Wesley's theology of history distanced itself to some degree from covenantal language and employed dispensational language in response to Calvinism. In addition, a theology of history validated two histories: firstly, it provided a clear, cogent view of history against the Calvinist doctrine of decrees, which seemed whether in the supralapsarian or the infralapsarian variety to militate against the significance and meaning of history. Secondly, it provided (particularly in Fletcher's thought) an order of salvation which

---

64. Deschner, 48, 57. In Wesley's *heilsgeschichte*, the exaltation of Christ encompasses the effusion of the Spirit. Unfortunately Lawrence Wood, in his work *The Meaning of Pentecost in Early Methodism*, fails to recognize in Wesley's *heilsgeschichte* the centrality of his Christological orientation.

65. Deschner, 45.

66. Wesley, *Explanatory Notes*, Rev. 5:7.

67. At times this was directed against what was perceived to be practical or theoretical antinomianism of Calvinists.

68. Wesley, *BE Works*, 2:27, 'The Law Established through Faith' (1750). Here Wesley states, 'Whereas now all good works, though as necessary as ever, are not antecedent to our acceptance, but consequent upon it' (ibid). Subsequently, he writes, 'Therefore that we are "justified by faith", even by "faith without works", is no ground for "making void the law through faith"; or for imagining that faith is a dispensation from any kind or degree of holiness' (ibid., 28). The moral law is not a condition of the believer's acceptance.

69. According to Deschner, the distinction made between the covenants and the dispensations is imprecise. See Deschner, 114.

further validated the personal histories of conversions. As William Cannon stated, 'The salvation of people takes place always within history, for people are the components of history, either those who make it or else have it made for them by others who lead them and cause them to fit into their grandiose schemes'.[70] Whereas the Calvinist morphology of conversion seemed to bypass the significance of personal histories of conversions due to its emphasis on divine fiat, Wesley's theology authenticated personal salvation experiences.

In his sermon, 'The Spirit of Bondage and Adoption' (1746), Wesley elucidates his morphology of conversion under the broad rubrics of 'natural man', 'legal man', and 'evangelical man'. Natural man has neither love nor fear of God; he neither conquers nor fights sin. The man in the legal state is awakened out of spiritual sleep through the law of God, sees his transgression of the law, and realizes the precarious state of life outside of Christ. In the third state, the evangelical man no longer experiences being under the law but is now under grace; he fights and conquers sin and experiences victory over sin through the reign of the Spirit in his life. Wesley's soteriology in this sermon focuses upon the subjective and existential aspects. Though his *ordo salutis* is similar in many respects to the Puritan scheme, his morphology of conversion differs from the common, Calvinistic Puritan morphology. William Perkins's 'golden chaine', which serves as a typical example includes predestination, calling, justification, sanctification and glorification.[71] Inherent in the Puritan scheme is a doctrine of divine providence 'whereby history was understood to be progressing in a straight line toward its intended goal under divine supervision. Within this providential order, they believed that God elected some to receive mercy and "interposed" in the normal course of affairs to preserve these individuals for salvation and then to lead them toward repentance and faith'.[72] Because Calvinistic morphologies of salvation were considered fatalistic, Wesley developed a theology of history which gave meaning to personal histories as well as the history of salvation within the world.

---

70. Cannon, 37.

71. Richard A. Muller, 'Perkins' *A Golden Chaine*: Predestinarian System or Schematized Ordo Salutis?', *Sixteenth Century Journal* 9, 1 (April 1978), 81.

72. D. B. Hindmarsh, 'The Olney Autobiographers; English Conversion Narrative in the Mid-Eighteenth Century', *Journal of Ecclesiastical History* 49, 1 (January 1998), 81.

Conclusion

In sum, what are the key features of Wesley's theology of history that were passed on to the early Methodists? First, it validated history, both general as well as personal history, against the Calvinistic doctrine of divine decrees and morphology of conversion which seemed to undermine the value or significance of history. Secondly, Wesley's theology of history provided a clear explanation of how the love of God included and an unlimited atonement applied to those who seemed to be excluded from the Calvinist doctrine of a limited atonement. It afforded, thirdly, a paradigm for progressive history which was concomitant with the optimism of grace and the doctrine of Christian perfection. In addition, Wesley's theology of history demonstrated the unity of the Testaments and the consistency of the salvific activity of God in every age of history, including the preservation of the validity of the moral law for Christians. Finally, it demonstrates the accommodation of God's revelation to humanity who at first concealed Himself so that human beings might better understand and move progressively to a greater knowledge of God.

BIBLICAL LANGUAGE
IN THE HYMNS OF CHARLES WESLEY

Randall D. McElwain

'Christians have been known as "people of the Book." Actually, we are a people of two books, the Bible and the hymnal.'[1] If Christians have been 'people
of two books', this was most certainly true of the people called Methodists.
Methodist families, even if they had no other personal library, owned at least
two books—a Bible and a hymnbook. The hymnbook provided their devotional reading, their guide to Christian growth, and their textbook of popular theology. Methodist laypeople learned both the Bible and their theology
through hymns, especially those of Charles Wesley.

  In spite of the fact that hymns were a primary medium by which
eighteenth-century Christians learned the Bible and theology, relatively little work has been done in analyzing the hermeneutical approach of hymn-
writers from the period. Considerable work has been done on John Wesley's
interpretation of scripture.[2] Much less attention has been given to Charles

---

1. Donald P. Hustad, *Jubilate II: Church Music in Worship and Renewal* (Carol Stream, IL, 1993),
447.

2. Scott J. Jones, *John Wesley's Conception and Use of Scripture* (Nashville, 1995); Robert Michael
Casto, 'Exegetical Method in John Wesley's *Explanatory Notes upon the Old Testament*: A Descrip-
tion of His Approach, Use of Sources, and Practice' (Ph.D. diss., Duke University, 1977); John
N. Oswalt, 'Wesley's Use of the Old Testament in His Doctrinal Teachings,' *Wesleyan Theological
Journal* 12 (1977): 39-51; William Arnett, 'John Wesley-Man of One Book: An Investigation of

Wesley's poetic hermeneutic. Some of the interpretive principles identified in Scott Jones's study of John Wesley's use of scripture can be seen in Charles Wesley's work as well.[3] Jones noted John Wesley's preference for using the words of scripture to interpret scripture. Wesley formulated this principle with the words of scripture: 'speak as the oracles of God.'[4] This principle is seen throughout Charles Wesley's work; whenever possible, Charles used the actual words of scripture in his hymns.

Charles's hymns also reflect his agreement with John's attempts to 'seek the most original text and the best translation.'[5] When Charles considered the King James translation inadequate, he substituted his own translation. One of the most famous examples is Wesley's use of Philippians 2:7 in the early hymn, 'Free Grace.' The Authorized Version states that Jesus 'made himself of no reputation....' Charles's more literal translation of the Greek text yielded the phrase '"emptied himself" of all but love.'[6]

> He left his Father's throne above
> (So free, so infinite his grace!)
> Emptied himself of all but love,
> And bled for *Adam's* helpless race:
> 'Tis mercy all, immense and free!
> For, O my God! it found out me![7]

To date, ST Kimbrough's 'Charles Wesley and Biblical Interpretation,'[8] an expansion of his earlier journal article on 'Charles Wesley as a Biblical Interpreter'[9] is the primary study of the younger Wesley's hermeneutical prin-

the Centrality of the Bible in the Life and Works of John Wesley with Special Emphasis on His Labours as an Interpreter of the New Testament' (Ph.D. diss., Drew University, 1954).

3. Jones, *John Wesley's Conception and Use of Scripture*.

4. Jones, *John Wesley's Conception and Use of Scripture*, 111.

5. Jones, *John Wesley's Conception and Use of Scripture*, 110.

6. John Lawson, *The Wesley Hymns as a Guide to Scriptural Teaching* (Grand Rapids, MI, 1987), 19; George Osborn, ed. *The Poetical Works of John and Charles Wesley*, 'Hymns and Sacred Poems, 1739' (London: Wesleyan-Methodist Conference Office, 1868-72), I:105-106.

7. Osborn, I:105-106.

8. ST Kimbrough, Jr., 'Charles Wesley and Biblical Interpretation', in Kimbrough (ed.), *Charles Wesley: Poet and Theologian* (Nashville, 1992), 106-136.

9. ST Kimbrough, Jr., 'Charles Wesley as a Biblical Interpreter', *Methodist History* 26/3 (April

ciples. Kimbrough examined currents in eighteenth-century biblical studies and identified important presuppositions that influenced Wesley's interpretive approach. These currents included an appreciation for biblical languages; the literal interpretation of the Reformers; and a greater recognition of the literary beauty of the Bible.[10] Kimbrough's analysis of Wesley's hermeneutic focused primarily on his unpublished short poems on scripture narratives. While these poems may not fully represent Charles Wesley's work as a whole, they represent one important aspect of his work. In these poems, Kimbrough saw a 'hermeneutic of imagination.'[11] This hermeneutic involves an experiential interpretation that allows the reader to 'reenact the initial experience of scripture', that transforms the scripture narrative into 'contemporaneous experience', and that creates a 'metamorphosis' in the reader.[12]

This essay examines Charles Wesley's use of scripture in hymns. It will argue that his varied approach to biblical language includes three contrasting uses of scripture. Some hymns allude to scriptural language in an almost casual fashion; some make explicit use of a biblical text without developing the passage; in other hymns, Wesley developed the text in sermonic form, much as a preacher might expound on a biblical passage.

Charles Wesley's hymns are saturated with scripture. In his analysis of fifty Wesley hymns, John Lawson found few lines that do not allude to the words of the Bible.[13] The Oxford edition of *A Collection of Hymns for the Use of the People Called Methodists* lists 2500 scripture references for the 525 hymns; allusions are made to every book of the Bible except Nahum and Philemon.[14] Because of Wesley's frequent use of scripture, a study of his approach to biblical interpretation is important for understanding his hymns. In addition to its importance for understanding his hymns, a study of Charles Wesley's biblical interpretation is important because of his influence on early Methodism. In spite of their sometimes tempestuous relationship, Charles

---

1988): 139-53.

10. ST Kimbrough, Jr., 'Charles Wesley and Biblical Interpretation', 107-112.

11. ST Kimbrough, Jr., Charles Wesley and Biblical Interpretation', 113.

12. ST Kimbrough, 'Charles Wesley and Biblical Interpretation', 114-120.

13. Lawson, *Wesley Hymns as a Guide.*

14. *A Collection of Hymns for the Use of the People Called Methodists,* vol. 7 of The Bicentennial Edition of the Works of John Wesley, ed. Franz Hildebrandt and Oliver A. Beckerlegge with James Dale (Oxford, 1983). Abbreviated *Collection* in the footnotes.

Wesley was an important influence on the early Methodist preachers.[15] Because of this, a study of his use of scripture will contribute to an understanding of early Methodist biblical interpretation.

Incidental Scriptural Allusions

In some instances, Charles Wesley used the words of the Bible because of their familiarity to himself and his audience. With this approach, the hymn's use of a biblical text is not directly related to its context; the language is simply a reflection of Wesley's intimate knowledge of the Bible.

Wesley's hymns reflect his studies of the early church fathers, classical literature, and English poets.[16] It was the Authorized Version of the Bible and the Psalter of the *Book of Common Prayer*, however, which provided the primary inspirations for his hymns. 'His familiarity, from a lifetime of devotional reading, enables him to speak in biblical phrases quite naturally.'[17] Certain biblical phrases appear regularly in Wesley's hymns, as if they were such a natural part of his vocabulary that they were constantly at hand. These include:

> 'Will not let thee go' from Genesis 32:26
> 'Stony heart' from Ezekiel 11:19
> 'Sun of righteousness' from Malachi 4:2.

Examples of Wesley's incidental use of biblical language can be seen in lines from 'For a Tender Conscience' published in the 1749 *Hymns and Sacred Poems*. The hymn is not based on one specific biblical text. Instead, it uses phrases that allude to various scripture passages:

> Almighty God of truth and love,　　　　　(Ps. 31:5)
> 　In me thy power exert,

---

15. John Lenton, 'Charles Wesley and the Preachers', in Kenneth G.C. Newport and Ted A. Campbell (ed.), *Charles Wesley: Life, Literature, & Legacy* (Peterborough, 2007), 88-108; Gareth Lloyd, *Charles Wesley and the Struggle for Methodist Identity* (Oxford, 2007), 111-119.

16. Frank Baker, *Charles Wesley's Verse: An Introduction* (London, 1964).

17. J.R. Watson, *The English Hymn: A Critical and Historical Study* (Oxford, 1999), 232.

The mountain from my soul remove,	(Mt. 17:20)
The hardness from my heart ...	(Mk. 16:14)

From thee that I no more may part,	
No more thy goodness grieve,	(Eph. 4:30; Rom. 2:4)
The filial awe, the fleshly heart,	(Ezek. 11:19)
The tender conscience give,	
Quick as the apple of an eye,	(Ps. 17:8; Prov. 7:2)
O God, my conscience make:	
Awake my soul, when sin is nigh,	(Gen. 4:7)
And keep it still awake.[18]	

None of these references are directly related to the topic of the hymn, and it is unlikely that Wesley consciously thought of each reference. It is more likely, as Henry Rack suggested, that 'the language of the hymns reveals a mind so steeped in the Bible as to use its language without conscious quotation.'[19]

The Oxford edition of *A Collection of Hymns for the Use of the People Called Methodists* includes an appendix that shows the allusions in a few representative hymns. In the sixteen lines of 'O thou who camest from above', there are twenty-five allusions, including:[20]

O thou who camest from above	(John 3:31)
The pure celestial fire t'impart,	(1 Kgs 18:39; Lk. 12:49)
Kindle a flame of sacred love	(1 Chr. 21:26)
On the mean altar of my heart!	(Lev. 9:24)
There let it for thy glory burn	(2 Cor. 4:15; 8:19)
With inextinguishable blaze,	(Lev. 6:13)
And trembling to its source return	(Job 5:7; Eccles. 2:7)
In humble love, and fervent praise.	(James 4:6, 10)

18. Charles Wesley, *Hymns and Sacred Poems,* 2 vols. (Bristol, 1749), II: 230-231.

19. Henry D. Rack, *Reasonable Enthusiast: John Wesley and the Rise of Methodism* (London, 1989), 257.

20. *Collection,* 733.

Wesley was so attuned to scripture that his poetry speaks this language as naturally as we speak the language of public discourse today. He 'had only one language, the language of Zion. The scriptures were his native tongue.'[21] Because of this, the careful reader often encounters lines that are reminiscent of the words of scripture, even when no direct allusion may be intended.

Intertextual Use of Scripture

While some scripture language in Wesley's hymns appears to be an incidental result of his vast biblical vocabulary, other hymns suggest conscious allusions to texts that parallel the message of the hymn. In these hymns, he used the words and narratives of scripture to mediate a biblical message to his contemporaries. A great hymn does much more than simply quote scripture or tie together isolated lines into a 'mosaic of biblical allusions.'[22] Rather, a hymn is a 'hermeneutic act. It takes a text, or an event, and interprets it, uses it, re-reads it, makes something new from it.'[23] This interpretive approach is seen in the intertextual use of biblical passages in many Wesley hymns.

Intertextuality is more than the casual use of Bible language; these deliberate allusions represent an effort to echo scripture in hymns. Wesley's use of scripture in this way is related to the echoes of the Hebrew Bible seen in many Pauline passages. In Deuteronomy 30:11-14, Moses told the people of Israel that the Law is near, not far removed and impossible to attain. Echoing Moses, Paul used similar language in Romans 10:6-8 to argue that 'the word of faith' has been brought near. Richard Hays, adapting the literary approach of John Hollander, argued that Paul is using 'intertextuality', the 'imbedding of fragments of an earlier text within a later one.'[24]

Intertextual fragments may be used in circumstances different from the original context. Hays traced Paul's language in Philippians 1:19[25] to

---

21. J. Ellsworth Kalas, *Our First Song: Evangelism in the Hymns of Charles Wesley* (Nashville, 1985), 24.

22. Henry Bett, *The Hymns of Methodism in their Literary Relations* (London, 1913), 16.

23. J.R. Watson, 'Pitying Tenderness and Tenderest Pity: The Hymns of Charles Wesley and the Writings of St Luke (The A.S. Peake Memorial Lecture)', *Epworth Review* 32/3 (2005), 33.

24. Richard B. Hays, *Echoes of Scripture in the Letters of Paul* (New Haven, CT, 1989), 1.

25. '... for I know that through your prayers and the help given by the Spirit of Jesus Christ, what has happened to me will turn out for my deliverance' (NIV).

Job's testimony in Job 13:16.[26] There is no citation formula, the allusion is fleeting, and 'Paul's sentence is entirely comprehensible to a reader who has never heard of Job.'[27] The reader who recognizes Paul's echo of Job, however, will find that the two passages resonate with each other. Paul is a prisoner; Job depicted himself as a prisoner (Job 13:27). Paul's statement comes as he awaits trial, confident that good will come, regardless of the results of the trial because, 'For to me to live is Christ, and to die is gain' (Phil. 1:21). Similarly, Job's statement comes in the context of his desire for a 'trial' before God, a trial that will result in his vindication (Job 13:18). An awareness of Paul's use of Job is not necessary to understanding Paul's message; but, the intertextual echo creates a 'counterpoint' in which a 'range of resonant harmonics become audible.'[28] Paul does not call attention to his use of Job, but his use of Job is significant to his message.

Paul's intertextuality is paralleled in Wesley's use of biblical language; Wesley repeatedly imbedded fragments of the biblical text in his writing. These are more than biblical allusions; they represent an attempt to echo the biblical context in Wesley's eighteenth-century world. This intertextuality allowed Wesley to express his own ideas in the language of scripture, and, for the careful reader, hints at parallels with the biblical setting from which these fragments are drawn.

In his *Journal,* Charles Wesley often alluded to biblical passages that paralleled contemporary events. On 7 July 1751 he 'Lodged at Mr E-------, who did run well,' an allusion to Paul's condemnation of those who abandoned the gospel after initial faith in Christ (Gal. 5:7).[29] A text communicating Paul's disillusionment with the Galatian backsliders is echoed in Wesley's entry showing his disappointment regarding Mr. E----'s backsliding. Similarly, Wesley quoted 2 Timothy 3:5 in an entry criticizing his Georgia parishioners who 'have more of the form of godliness than the power.'[30] Citing a phrase from Judges 21:25, he wrote of the refusal of a constable to protect

---

26. 'Indeed, this will turn out for my deliverance, for no godless man would dare come before him' (NIV).

27. Hays, *Echoes of Scripture,* 21.

28. Hays, *Echoes of Scripture,* 23.

29. Charles Wesley, *The Manuscript Journal of the Reverend Charles Wesley, M.A.,* ed. S T Kimbrough, Jr. and Kenneth G.C. Newport, 2 vols. (Nashville, TN, 2008), I: xxi.

30. Wesley, *Journal,* I:14.

Methodists from rioters, 'As there is no king in Israel (no magistrate, I mean in Sheffield), every man does as seems good in his eyes.'[31] The journals are replete with such biblical allusions.

　　In a letter to Vincent Perronet during the aftermath of the Grace Murray affair, Charles expressed his astonishment that John did not take blame for the fiasco. Charles wrote, 'I declared I would cover his nakedness as long as I could [Gen. 9:23], and honour him before the people [I Sam. 15:30]'.[32] Given Charles's extreme reaction to the marriage proposal, one can imagine that he saw John as both the drunken, shameful Noah and the divinely rejected Saul in the relevant passages. Wesley used the same technique in his hymns. He wrote:

> O that thou wouldst the heavens rent,
> 　　In majesty come down;
> Stretch out thine arm omnipotent,
> 　　And seize me for thine own.[33]

With this, he accomplishes two things: he adapts the familiar words of Isaiah 64:1 for his personal prayer for revival and, more directly, he relates his need for freedom from sin's chains to Israel's historic prayer for deliverance from captivity. Only God could deliver Israel from their enemies; only God can break sin's power. Wesley continues:

> What though I cannot break my chain,
> 　　Or e'er throw off my load!
> The things impossible to men
> 　　Are possible to God.

In a hymn 'for believers fighting', Wesley alludes to Exodus 33:20. On Mount Sinai, God told Moses 'You cannot see my face; for no one shall see me and live.' Wesley uses this language to suggest his deep hunger for a true knowledge of God. Wesley set himself in Moses' dilemma and replied:

31. Wesley, *Journal*, II:345.
32. Wesley, *Journal*, II:358.
33. *Collection*, Hymn 134.

> I cannot see thy face, and live,
> Then let me see thy face, and die!
> Now, Lord, my gasping spirit receive,
> Give me on eagles' wings to fly,
> With eagles' eyes on thee to gaze,
> And plunge into the glorious blaze.[34]

The literary scholar Reuben Brower stated that his purpose in studying allusion in Alexander Pope was 'to see how he used the poetry of the past for his own expressive purposes.'[35] In the same way, a study of intertextual allusion in Wesley's hymns shows his use of scripture to express his own theological and devotional thoughts.

Sermonic Development of Biblical Texts

Like his contemporaries, Charles Wesley saw himself as a preacher more than as a poet.[36] He 'did not think of himself primarily as a poet; in hymn as in homily, he was a Methodist preacher.'[37] Perhaps Wesley's most interesting use of scripture is his use of biblical passages as texts for hymnic sermons. This approach to biblical interpretation is similar to the sermonic exposition of the Old Testament seen in the Epistle to the Hebrews.[38] Phrases from the scripture text are developed and expounded in each stanza.

Wesley's 'Jubilee Hymn' from 'Hymns for New Year's Day, MDCCL' illustrates this sermonic approach to biblical interpretation in hymns. The hymn is based on the commands and promises of Leviticus 25:8-17. The Law of the Year of Jubilee required Israelites to restore land to the original owner every fiftieth year. This encouraged social justice, limited avarice, and protected the poor. When Israel failed to observe this law, the prophets thundered God's condemnation:

---

34. *Collection*, Hymn 275.

35. Quoted in Hays, *Echoes of Scripture*, 19.

36. Kenneth G.C. Newport, *The Sermons of Charles Wesley: A Critical Edition* (Oxford, 2001), 47.

37. John R. Tyson, *Charles Wesley on Sanctification* (Grand Rapids, MI, 1986), 22.

38. Gareth L. Cockerill, *Hebrews: A Bible Commentary in the Wesleyan Tradition* (Indianapolis, IN, 1999), 12-13.

Therefore because you trample on the poor and take from them lev-
ies of grain, you have built houses of hewn stone, but you shall not
live in them; you have planted pleasant vineyards, but you shall not
drink their wine. For I know how many are your transgressions, and
how great are your sins-- you who afflict the righteous, who take a
bribe, and push aside the needy in the gate.[39]

The law of Jubilee was a command; it also implied a promise. If Israel maintained a just society, if they protected the patrimony which God had given
them, and if they were faithful to God's commands, God would make the
Year of Jubilee a year of restoration, Sabbath rest, and celebration. The trumpet blast of Leviticus 25:9 signalled a year of rejoicing.

In his sermon at Nazareth, Jesus applied this imagery to his own ministry.[40] After centuries of exile, prophetic silence, and subjugation to foreign
dominance, Jesus sounded a trumpet call that promised the return of Jubilee.
Through his ministry, those in exile would be restored, the blind would see,
and those who suffered oppression would be freed. Wesley followed Jesus
in recognizing the implied messianic promise in the Year of Jubilee text. The
blast of the *shofar* became the blast of the 'gospel trumpet.' And, like Luke,
Wesley read Jesus' proclamation as more than physical restoration; he saw
the fulfilment of the Year of Jubilee in the spread of the good news of spiritual
restoration to all humankind:

> Blow ye the trumpet, blow,
> The gladly solemn sound,
> Let all the nations know,
> To earth's remotest bound;
> The year of Jubilee is come!
> Return, ye ransomed sinners, home.
>
> Jesus, our great High-priest,
> Hath full atonement made:
> Ye weary spirits, rest,

39. Amos 5:11-12 (NIV).
40. Luke 4:16-27.

Ye mournful souls, be glad;
The year of Jubilee is come!
Return, ye ransomed sinners, home.

The gospel trumpet hear,
The news of heavenly grace,
And, saved from earth, appear
Before your Saviour's face:
The year of Jubilee is come!
Return, ye ransomed sinners, home.[41]

Illustrating his sermonic approach to interpretation, Wesley's hymn on Deuteronomy 6:7 closely follows the structure of the biblical text. Wesley applied the ancient text to the life of the singer today. The Mosaic text noted four occasions for teaching the Law in Jewish families:

And thou shalt teach them diligently unto thy children,
and shalt talk of them when thou sittest in thine house,
and when thou walkest by the way,
and when thou liest down,
and when thou risest up.

These four phrases provide the structure for Wesley's hymn. Each phrase of the biblical text inspired a meditation on the believer's practice of God's presence. On the phrase 'When thou sittest in thine house', Wesley wrote:

When quiet in my house I sit,
    Thy book be my companion still
My joy thy sayings to repeat,
    Talk o'er the records of thy will,

And search the oracles divine,
Till every heartfelt word be mine.

---

41. Osborn, ed. *Poetical Works*, 'Hymns for New Year's Day, MDCCL', VI:12.

On the phrase 'When thou walkest by the way', he wrote:
> O might the gracious words divine
>> Subject of all my converse be!
>
> So will the Lord his follower join,
>> And walk and talk himself with me,
>
> So would my heart his presence prove,
> And burn with everlasting love.

On the phrase 'When thou liest down', he wrote:
> Oft as I lay me down to rest,
>> O may the reconciling word
>
> Sweetly compose my weary breast!
>> While, on the bosom of my Lord,
>
> I sink in blissful dreams away,
> And visions of eternal day.

The phrase 'When thou risest up' concludes the hymn:
> Rising to sing my Saviour's praise,
>> Thee may I publish all day long;
>
> And let thy precious word of grace
>> Flow from my heart, and fill my tongue
>
> Fill all my life with purest love,
> And join me to thy church above.[42]

In a manner consistent with the biblical interpretation of his time, Wesley took a text from the Hebrew Bible, interpreted it christologically, and applied it to the daily experience of the Christian believer to whom he writes.

Another hymn which reflects Charles Wesley's christological interpretation of the Old Testament is 'Wrestling Jacob' from Genesis 32:24-32. In this hymn, one that Isaac Watts considered Wesley's greatest,[43] the Jacob narrative is seen as a typology of Christian experience. Wesley 'takes the experience of Jacob wrestling with the angel and presents it as the story of

---

42. Charles Wesley, *Short Hymns on Select Passages of the Holy Scriptures*, 2 vols. (Bristol, 1762), I:92-93.

43. Glenn Clark, 'Charles Wesley's Greatest Poem,' *Methodist History*, 26/3 (April 1988), 168.

the agony and joy of every truly repentant and eventually justified sinner.'[44] 'Wrestling Jacob' is not a verse by verse exegesis of the scripture. Rather, Wesley 'transform(s) the imagery of scripture into categories of contemporaneous experience.'[45] This is a hymnic sermon in which the singer is not just an observer but a participant in the narrative:

> Charles intended not only to communicate biblical teaching, but also to cause us to replicate biblical experience. ...he turned the singer of his hymns into an actor in the biblical drama he is recounting. By singing Wesley's poetical renditions of Scripture, we become "wrestling Jacob," struggling for "the blessing".[46]

This hymn shows the experiential emphasis of Charles Wesley's interpretation of the Old Testament narrative:

> Come, O thou Traveller unknown,
> 　　　Whom still I hold, but cannot see!
> My company before is gone,
> 　　　And I am left alone with thee;
> With thee all night I mean to stay,
> 　　　And wrestle till the break of day.
>
> I need not tell thee who I am,
> 　　　My misery and sin declare;
> Thyself hast called me by my name,
> 　　　Look on thy hands, and read it there;
> But who, I ask thee, who art Thou?
> 　　　Tell me Thy name, and tell me now.
>
> In vain thou strugglest to get free,
> 　　　I never will unloose my hold!

---

44. T. Crichton Mitchell, *Charles Wesley: Man with the Dancing Heart* (Kansas City, MO, 1994), 245.

45. ST Kimbrough, Jr., 'Charles Wesley and Biblical Interpretation', 118.

46. Tyson, *Charles Wesley*, 25.

Art thou the Man that died for me?
   The secret of thy love unfold;
Wrestling, I will not let thee go,
Till I thy name, thy nature know.

Wilt thou not yet to me reveal
   Thy new, unutterable name?
Tell me, I still beseech thee, tell;
   To know it now resolved I am;
Wrestling, I will not let thee go,
Till I thy name, thy nature know.

Yield to me now, for I am weak,
   But confident in self-despair;
Speak to my heart, in blessings speak,
   Be conquered by my instant prayer;
Speak, or thou never hence shalt move,
And tell me if thy name is Love.

'Tis Love! 'tis Love! thou diedst for me!
   I hear thy whisper in my heart;
The morning breaks, the shadows flee,
   Pure, universal love thou art;
To me, to all, thy bowels move;
Thy nature and thy name is Love.

The Sun of righteousness on me
   Hath rose with healing in his wings,
Withered my nature's strength; from thee
   My soul its life and succour brings;
My help is all laid up above;
Thy nature and thy name is Love.

Lame as I am, I take the prey,
   Hell, earth, and sin, with ease o'ercome;

> I leap for joy, pursue my way,
>   And as a bounding hart fly home,
> Through all eternity to prove
> Thy nature and thy name is Love.[47]

While this approach to scripture does not meet the expectations of twentieth-century historical-critical interpretation (although, interestingly, it is close to the twenty-first-century understanding of reader response theory), it is consistent with how poets and musicians have long treated scripture. ST Kimbrough recognized art as a form of biblical interpretation:

> Art functions best in living forms, and, hence, it approaches scripture within the context of life as it is lived, not merely as it has been lived. Johannes Brahms' musical setting of I Corinthians 13, for example, in the *Four Serious Songs* translates these words into a living covenant of present existence. Benjamin Britten has actualized the flood story of Genesis 6-9 in his church opera, *Nove's Fludde*, in a way never before accomplished by any biblical exegete.[48]

Conclusion

Wesley's use of biblical language suggests both the natural outflow of a lifetime of biblical study and a deliberate effort to 'preach' through his hymns. In his use of biblical language, Wesley moved between the incidental use of a familiar scripture vocabulary, deliberate intertextual allusions, and sermonic development of texts. Each of these approaches contributes to the great variety of biblical language in his hymns. Wesley's use of scripture does not indicate a struggle to locate proof texts that could be adapted to his hymns. Rather, he brings '"things new and old" out of the scriptures simply by absorbing them into his being and then writing and speaking.'[49]

    This essay is a first step in studying Charles Wesley's use of scripture. In a thesis on the theology of Charles Wesley's hymns, this author will ex-

---

47. *Collection*, Hymn 136.

48. Kimbrough, 'Charles Wesley as a Biblical Interpreter', 141.

49. Sister Benedicta, quoted in Timothy Dudley-Smith, 'Charles Wesley – A Hymnwriter for Today', *The Hymn* 39/4 (October, 1988): 11.

amine several principles that guided Wesley's interpretation of the Bible, including (1) christological interpretation, (2) experiential interpretation, and (3) poetic interpretation.[50] As Charles Wesley's interpretative approach is analyzed, scholars may gain new appreciation of an important voice in early Methodist biblical interpretation.

In the broader field of eighteenth-century hymnody, future research may include a comparative study of the use of scripture by other hymn writers. Isaac Watts,[51] Philip Doddridge,[52] John Newton,[53] and the Wesleys' rival, Augustus Toplady[54] each published collections of hymns that made extensive use of scripture. A comparison of these collections will show the range of biblical interpretation in eighteenth-century hymnody.

Hymns were central to the theological and biblical understanding of early Methodists, especially the laity. Because of this, the study of biblical interpretation in hymns will deepen our understanding of popular hermeneutics in early Methodism.

---

50. Randall D. McElwain, 'Doctrine in the Hymns of Charles Wesley: Three Theological Themes in the 1780 Collection of Hymns' (Ph.D. diss., University of Manchester (Nazarene Theological College), in progress).

51. Isaac Watts, *Hymns and Spiritual Songs*, 3 vols. (London, 1707).

52. Philip Doddridge, *Hymns Founded on the Various Texts in the Holy Scriptures* (London, 1755).

53. John Newton, *Olney Hymns*, 3 vols. (London, 1779).

54. Augustus Toplady, *Psalms and Hymns for Public and Private Worship* (London, 1776).

'THOU SHAL[T] WALK WITH ME IN WHITE': AFTERLIFE AND VOCATION IN THE MINISTRY OF MARY BOSANQUET FLETCHER

D. R. Wilson

'Your Society sanctions women's preaching, then?' 'It doesn't forbid them, sir, when they've a clear call to the work, and when their ministry is owned by the conversion of sinners and the strengthening of God's people. Mrs Fletcher, as you may have heard about, was the first woman to preach in the Society, I believe, before she was married, when she was Miss Bosanquet; and Mr Wesley approved of her undertaking the work. She had a great gift, and there are many others now living who are precious fellow-helpers in the work of the ministry. I understand there's been voices raised against it in the Society of late, but I cannot but think their counsel will come to nought. It isn't for men to make channels for God's Spirit, as they make channels for the water-courses and say, "Flow here, but flow not there."'

-Dinah Morris in George Eliot's *Adam Bede*[1]

This essay explores the relationship of Mary Fletcher's (née Bosanquet, 1739-1815) theology concerning the afterlife to her vocation. Mary was raised in the Church of England, catechized as a child by her father, confirmed in St Paul's Cathedral (*c*.1753), and had a progressive experience of conversion over the next four years, during which she attended Anglican worship and

---

1. George Eliot, *Adam Bede* (London: Penguin, 2008), 98.

Methodist society meetings.[2] During the fifty years following her conversion, Mary engaged in a variety of ministries, which included establishing a religious community of women,[3] founding an orphanage, becoming one of the first female Methodist preachers, and playing a central role in the ministry of a local Anglican parish. It is the argument of this essay that belief in the afterlife and concern for the unconverted, intrinsic to evangelical faith,[4] was appropriated by Fletcher to expand and sustain her vocational ministry in an environment in which, as David Hempton has observed, 'Women were able to exploit the sheer pragmatism of evangelical religion . . . as they moved from more confined to more expansive circles of influence without

2. Ms. Autobiography of Mary Bosanquet Fletcher [hereafter: AMBF], Methodist Archives and Research Centre, John Rylands University Library of Manchester [hereafter: MARC], Fletcher-Tooth Collection [hereafter FTC], MAM Fl. 23/1, p. 11-18. Whenever possible, quotations from Mary Bosanquet Fletcher's autobiography are taken from manuscript originals in Mary Fletcher's hand, rather than Henry Moore's edition, *The Life of Mrs. Mary Fletcher, Consort and Relict of the Rev. John Fletcher, Vicar of Madeley, Salop* (Birmingham: J. Peart and Son, 1817). Moore heavily edited Mary Fletcher's manuscripts and thus, the originals provide us with a less-altered picture of her life. Citations from Moore's edition are referred to hereafter as: Moore, *Life of Mrs. Fletcher*.

3. Mary Bosanquet's 'religious community', which she referred to as her 'family', was modelled after that of A.H. Francke's community and orphanage at Halle. See AMBF, MARC, FTC, MAM Fl. 23/1, p. 11-12, 23. On 1 December 1764 John Wesley, after visiting Mary Bosanquet's small community of women and their orphanage at Leytonstone, remarked, 'M. B. gave me a farther account of their affairs at Leytonstone. It is exactly *Pietas Hallensis* in miniature.' J. Wesley, *Works of John Wesley*, 3rd edn. T. Jackson, ed. (London, 1879), 3: 201, 11: 333 [hereafter: *WJW* (J)]. Wesley was also keen to compare her community to that of Ferrar at Little Gidding. See, J. Wesley, *A Short Account of the Life and Death of the Rev. John Fletcher, Vicar of Madeley* (New York, NY, 1805), 94-95. On the Halle model and pietism in England, see Daniel L. Brunner, *Halle Pietists in England: Anthony William Boehm and the Society for Promoting Christian Knowledge*, Arbeiten Zur Geschichte Des Pietismus, vol. 29, K. Aland, E. Peschke and G. Schäfer, eds. (Göttingen, 1988). Mary Fletcher's reference to her community as her 'family' was not unconventional, though the religious connotation incited some to accuse her of attempting to raise her orphans as nuns. See S. Burder, *Memoirs of Eminently Pious Women of the British Empire*, vol. 3 (London, 1823), 383-84. On 'family' in the eighteenth century, see N. Tadmor, *Family and Friends in Eighteenth-Century England: Household, Kinship, and Patronage* (Cambridge, 2001), 21-43, 167-68, 198-215.

4. D. Bebbington's quadrilateral of evangelical characteristics serves as the basis for what I mean by 'evangelical' in this paper. See *Evangelicalism in Modern Britain: A History from the 1730s to the 1980s* (London, 1988), 1-19. For a presentation of the view of evangelicalism as having origins in and continuity with later seventeenth-century Anglicans, see G. Hammond, 'The Revival of Practical Christianity: the Society for Promoting Christian Knowledge, Samuel Wesley, and the Clerical Society Movement', in Kate Cooper and Jeremy Gregory (ed.), *Revival and Resurgence in Christian History*, Studies in Church History 44 (Woodbridge, 2008), 116-27.

ever being able to redraw boundaries altogether.'[5] This inability to establish permanence in the enlargement of spheres of female influence has led some to conclude that evangelical women in the eighteenth century failed 'to practice real agency by resisting male domination and the social convention that ladies should be passive in private and modest in public.'[6] In contrast to this negative view, I contend that Mary Fletcher's theology of the afterlife, rooted in her evangelical faith, aided her in sustaining a lifetime of ministry.

A burgeoning interest in the religious experience and vocational work of early modern women over the last two decades has produced a number of useful studies for understanding the religious roles of women as leaders, preachers, dreamers, teachers, wives, mothers, mystics, visionaries, and missionaries.[7] However, the extent to which belief in the afterlife shaped women's sense of vocation and provided ongoing agency has been given less attention, partially due to feminist critiques of religion which emphasize autonomy as the central characteristic of agency.[8] In contrast to these critiques, Phyllis Mack has urged scholars to consider, 'a conception of agency in which autonomy is less important than self-transcendence and in which the energy to act in the world is generated and sustained by a prior act of per-

---

5. D. Hempton, *The Religion of the People: Methodism and Popular Religion c. 1750-1900* (London, 1996), 180.

6. As summarized by P. Mack, 'Religion, Feminism, and the Problem of Agency: Reflections on Eighteenth-Century Quakerism', *Signs: Journal of Women in Culture and Society*, 29:1 (2003), 154 [hereafter: Mack, 'Religion']. For helpful analysis of the private and public spheres of women in relation to the Evangelical Revival, see L. Davidoff and C. Hall, *Family Fortunes: Men and Women of the English Middle Class 1780-1850* (London, 1987), esp. pp. 74-76, 88-106, 114-117. Also see Jeremy Gregory's similar note on how the religious ideals of Mary Astell and Hannah More inspired and sustained them. 'Writing Women in(to) the Long Eighteenth Century', *Literature and History*, third series, 11:1 (Spring 2002), 85.

7. On evangelicalism and dreams, visions, and belief in the supernatural, see A. Taves, *Fits, Trances and Visions: Experiencing Religion and Explaining Experience from Wesley to James* (Princeton, NJ, 1999), 13-75. G.M. Jantzen's book, *Power, Gender and Mysticism*, though focused on the medieval period, is a useful starting point for revising our understanding of how women mystics have found agency in experience despite male-defined boundaries. (Cambridge, 1995), esp. pp. 157-192; also see P. Mack, *Visionary Women: Ecstatic Prophecy in Seventeenth-Century England* (Berkeley, CA, 1992); P.W. Chilcote, *John Wesley and the Women Preachers of Early Methodism* (Lanham, MD, 1991). A. Stott, 'Women and Religion', in *Women's History: Britain, 1700-1850 An Introduction*, H. Barker and E. Chalus, eds. (London and New York, 2005), 100-123; S. Mendelson and P. Crawford, *Women in Early Modern England 1550-1720* (Oxford, 1998), 225-241.

8. Mack, 'Religion', 149-154.

sonal surrender.'[9] It is this concept of agency which was practiced by Mary
Fletcher, and I suggest, was undergirded by her eschatological belief.

Throughout the eighteenth century, death was an eminent concern.
Life expectancy at birth was 37 years in 1750 and descended to 35 years by
1781,[10] a period during which consumption (i.e., pulmonary tuberculosis),
fevers, and smallpox were the cause of 43.4 per cent of deaths.[11] W.M. Jacob
has pointed out that 'At every level of society there was an awareness of the
brevity of life', which 'helped to focus their thoughts on eternity'.[12] Even so,
Kenneth Newport has shown that it has been common in histories of Methodism to gloss over or take for granted the significance of eschatological belief in the eighteenth century.[13] Although Newport focused largely upon millenarianism, his point that there was within 'British Methodism a strong and
recurrent streak of vivid eschatological interest',[14] is important regarding the
overall concern for life after death, which provided an impetus for preaching
the gospel. Conversion was inherently teleological, and the post-conversion
line between calling to a holy or perfect[15] life, and calling to ministerial service was often perceived as one and the same. For many converts, the very experience of conversion inspired a sense of mission and duty to proclaim the
'gospel' message in public. Many men who experienced this sense of calling
were prompted to pursue ordination in the Established Church or a dissent-
ing sect or to become a lay preacher within the various Methodisms of the
period.[16] However, neither of these options were available to women who

9. Ibid., 156.

10. E.A. Wrigley and R.S. Schofield, *The Population History of England 1541-1871: A Reconstruc-
tion* (Cambridge, 1989), 140, 150, 251, and passim.

11. J. Landers, 'Table 1: Contribution (%) of causes of death to total burials', in 'Historical Epi-
demiology and the Structural Analysis of Mortality', *Health Transition Review* 2 (1992), 53. I owe
this reference to Lisa Wilson.

12. W.M. Jacob, *Lay People and Religion in the Early Eighteenth Century* (Cambridge, 1996), 14,
[hereafter: Jacob, *Lay People and Religion*].

13. K.G.C. Newport, 'Methodists and the Millennium: Eschatological Expectation and the Interpretation of Biblical Prophecy in Early British Methodism', *Bulletin of the John Rylands University Library of Manchester* 78:1 (Spring 1996), 103-122.

14. Ibid., 104.

15. Greek: τέλειος.

16. See J.B. Sheldon, 'Hill's Arrangement', *Proceedings of the Wesley Historical Society*, 30 (1955-
56); J.H. Lenton, 'My Sons in the Gospel: An Analysis of Wesley's Itinerant Preachers', *Wesley
Historical Society Lecture* (Wesley Historical Society, 2000). Also, it is important to note that vo-

had experienced the same vocational call in their own lives, and those who claimed such a call were most commonly regarded with scepticism if not utter disdain.[17]

Neither the Established Church nor Methodism as a movement within the Church, offered the opportunity for women to pursue a call to either lay or ordained preaching. This presented a theological and practical challenge for women, who as their converted male counterparts, felt a sincere call to simply relate 'what [G]od had done for her soul'.[18] As Paul Chilcote has noted of women in the early Evangelical Revival, 'The initial adherents to the evangelical message preached by Wesley and his itinerants . . . were very often women. . . Some women took the initiative in the actual formation of societies with no other authority than their own determination and sense of divine calling.'[19] After an experience of conviction under the teaching of Sarah Crosby, reputedly the first woman preacher of Methodism,[20] Mary wrote, 'the prospect of a Life wholy [*sic*] devoted to God drank up every other [prospect]'.[21] But her call was not only towards a life of holiness but towards an active pursuit of vocational service *in the Church*:

cational ministry was not the only sphere of religious action in which we can observe eighteenth century piety and ministerial practice. See Jacob, *Lay People and Religion*. Reference here to 'various Methodisms' suggests that Methodism in the eighteenth century was by no means monolithic, but rather was manifested quite differently in various localities, particularly when we look to the parishes of England. For example, in Madeley, where John Fletcher, who repeatedly refused John Wesley's request that he leave his parish to succeed him as the leader of the Methodists, carried on his own parish 'Methodism', building meeting houses and schools that were functionally adjunct to the church. Mary Fletcher carried on her husband's 'Church Methodism' in Madeley for thirty years after his death, demonstrating that even after the Deed of Declaration (1784) and after Wesley's death (1791), Anglicanism still proved flexible enough in some areas to resist the separationist trend. In addition to local variations there were theological ones such as the divide over 'perfection' and over Calvinist or Arminian doctrine. This issue has been taken up by David Hempton, *Methodism: Empire of the Spirit* (New Haven, CT, 2005), and hinted at in Henry Rack, 'Some Recent Trends in Wesley Scholarship', *Wesleyan Theological Journal* 41:2 (Fall 2006), 184-199. Also see Gareth Lloyd, *Charles Wesley and the Struggle for Methodist Identity* (Oxford, 2007), esp. pp. x, 64-66.

17. Cf. Moore, *Life of Mrs. Fletcher*, 1:145; also see Z. Taft, *Biographical Sketches of the Lives and Public Ministry of Various Holy Women*, 2 vols. (London, 1825-28).

18. AMBF, MARC, FTC, MAM Fl. 23/1, p. 18. Mary Bosanquet was in this instance referring to Sarah Crosby.

19. Chilcote, *John Wesley*, 50.

20. Ibid.; D. Hempton, *Methodism: Empire of the Spirit*, 142.

21. AMBF, MARC, FTC, MAM Fl. 23/1, p. 18.

> I have ... seen the path very clear in w^h I ought to walk ... the Lord
> seems *to call me out* to more activity insomuch that I am ready to cry
> out ["]Lord what wilt thou have me to do?" ... my <u>firm resolution</u> is
> to be wholy [*sic*] given up *to the church* in any way he pleases.[22]

Thou Shal[t] Walk with Me in White

Mary's conviction that she should be given up 'to the church' continued and
she remained faithful in her attendance in the Established Church throughout her life. Several images held particular importance for her as she began
exploring where God was calling her. The first image came to her in a vision
which she received later in the year during a period of self-doubt and spiritual
crisis. As she recorded it many years later: 'my mind was greatly deprest I co^d
find no comfort from any kind Either in [G]od or outward things.'[23] This trial
became a pivotal moment for her vocationally. Up to this point she had been
supported by like-minded friends, co-converts who 'united in order to pray
together, to receive the word of exhortation, and to watch over one another
in love ... to work out their salvation.'[24] Seventeen years old, and seeking affirmation, she lay in her room reflecting and 'weeping before the Lord'.[25] In
that moment, just at her time of need,[26] she perceived the following vision:

> I deserND an unusual Brightness ... & from that bright cloud came a
> voice so powerfull that I can only say I heard it with <u>every faculty</u> of
> soul & body: it penetrated me thro & thro: with those words '<u>thou
> shall walk with me in White</u>.'[27] [T]he answer seemd to come from

---

22. Letter of Mary Bosanquet to Sarah Crosby, 17 May 1757, copied in by Bosanquet in AMBF, MAM Fl. 23/1, p. 19; underlining in the original; italics mine.

23. ABMF, MARC, FTC, MAM Fl. 23/1, p. 23.

24. John Wesley, 'The Nature, Design, and General Rules of the United Societies', in *The Works of John Wesley*, Bicentennial Edition, vol. 9, ed. by Rupert E. Davies (Nashville, TN, 1989), 69.

25. AMBF, MARC: MAM Fl. 23/1, p.23.

26. On the timeliness of dreams and visions in providing spiritual comfort and agency, see Phyl-lis Mack, 'Agency and the Unconscious: The Methodist Culture of Dreaming', in *Heart Religion in the British Enlightenment: Gender and Emotion in Early Methodism* (Cambridge, 2008), 219ff.

27. Rev. 3:4.

my heart as independent of myself 'Lord how can that be, seeing I am not worthy?' [I]t was spoke to me again '<u>but thou shall walk w^h me in White for I will make thee worthy</u>.'[28]

Thus recorded Mary Fletcher a theophany which was to provide her with both a vocational trajectory and a theological affirmation of that calling throughout her ministry. The image of walking with God in white was taken from Revelation 3:4 and was a reminder to hold fast and watch for Jesus who would return 'as a thief, and thou shalt not know what hour I will come upon thee.'[29] The promise was eschatological, pointing to the consummation of her life and calling. Thus, it provided Mary with affirmation rooted in her belief in the life to come. It provided her, first, with experiential evidence that her conversion was real, and second, with a conviction that her sense of vocation was part of God's plan. Eternity (a better word for expressing the meaning than 'afterlife') was impinging upon the present and had immediate and practical relevance for her. The next lines she wrote were from a hymn by Charles Wesley and reveal her interpretation of the promise she received in her vision: 'Everlasting Life is won—glory is on earth begun.'[30]

Rather than a 'chiliasm of the defeated and the hopeless',[31] her eschatological belief provided hope for eternity as well as empowerment to act in the sphere to which God had called her in the present. Such empowerment came to her in a vision shortly before she first preached in Bristol. She had prayed: 'Well, do all thy will, so I may but feel *that promise* accomplished'[32] Throughout her life, the image of God's promise that she would walk with him in white provided her with hope, and writing towards the end of her life, Mary wrote: 'To this day I have the most lively remembrance of that manifestation; and in the darkest moments I have since passed through, I could never doubt its being the voice of the Lord.'[33]

28. AMBF, MARC, FTC, MAM Fl. 23/1, pp. 23-24, underlining in the original.

29. Rev. 3:3 (AV).

30. This stanza is from the hymn by Charles Wesley, 'Hymn After the Sacrament', and quoted by John Wesley in his sermon 'Sermon 7: The Way to the Kingdom', in *The Works of John Wesley*, Bicentennial Edition, vol. 1, ed. by Albert C. Outler (Nashville, TN, 1984), 217-234.

31. E.P. Thompson, *The Making of the English Working Class* (Harmondsworth, 1968), 419.

32. Moore, *Life of Mrs. Fletcher*, 1: 121; emphasis mine.

33. MARC, FTC, MAM Fl. 23/1, p. 24.

A Stranger and a Foreigner

As Anne Stott has noted, 'the Bible . . . gave women a language to validate their callings'.[34] A common biblical image appropriated by Mary Fletcher was that of 'strangers and foreigners'. At the age of 17 she was convicted that 'plainness of dress & behaviour best became a Christian',[35] and heeding this, she decided so to act in surrender, that she might consider herself such 'a stranger and a foreigner'.[36] By freeing herself from material things, she believed she could carry out a ministry which aligned her with the 'strangers and pilgrims' of the New Testament Epistle to the Hebrews, which exhorted believers to be encouraged by 'a cloud of witnesses',[37] heroes of faith from the Old Testament. Like Abraham, who was called out of the land of Ur to a land that God would show him, Mary saw herself as being called out of the world to a life of holiness. The encouragement of a 'cloud of witnesses' now in glory as co-pilgrims and co-strangers who had experienced God's provision, also instructed her in her calling. Her own identification with strangers gave her an empathy for the poor of the earth, giving rise to her establishment of an orphanage: 'I felt the same desire I had done at that time to become in any or every [sense] a servant of the Church[.] [T]hose words were still with me "if she hath Lodged Strangers, if she have brought up Children; if she have relieved the afflicted & Dilligently followd after every good work."'[38]

Borders and Habitations

Another biblical image which built upon that of 'strangers and foreigners' was that of 'borders and habitations'. When Mary had first taken up 'plainness of dress', her parents considered it extreme, and Mary herself considered the possibility that it would make her look strange in the eyes of the world, and could result in hardship. However, appropriating again a biblical image, she wrote, borrowing a phrase from the Book of Acts that sets the stage of human life in eternal perspective: 'I believe the <u>Lord appoints the bounds of our</u>

34. A. Stott, 'Women and Religion', 102.

35. MARC, FTC, MAM Fl. 23/1, p.26.

36. Ibid.

37. Heb. 12:1.

38. MARC, FTC, MAM Fl. 23/1, p. 11.

<u>habitation</u> & that no good thing shall be witheld [*sic*] from those who walk uprightly. I have therefore nothing to do but to commend my self to God by holy obedience & leave every step of my life to be guided by his will.'[39] In so much as she saw herself as being 'not of the world', so she saw her habitation in eternity. This provided her with a sense of authority when challenged by her critics who saw her willingness to take the poor into her house as a sign of irresponsibility and foolishness. '[S]ome objected' she wrote, 'your income is as yet but small—you wish to be usefull, wh[y] then did you not chuse as a friend, one who had some fortune to unite w^h your own & that might have *inlarged your sphere.*['] I answerd I did not <u>chuse</u> at all—I stood still, saw, & followd ye order of God--& if my *sphere had been inlarged* in money and Lessend in grace what should I have gaind by that?'[40]

Following the example of Jabez in 1 Chronicles 4:10, Mary Fletcher prayed throughout her life that God would enlarge her habitation, by which she referred to her sphere of ministry activity.[41] By 1795—then living in the parish of Madeley—Mary had established an extensive parish ministry: preaching, meeting classes of men, women, and children, and drawing clergy from nearby parishes to hear her.[42] Yet, doubts still arose in her mind. Once again, reflecting on the heavenly habitation of eternity, the imagery of 'desiring a better country' or of 'enlarged borders' provided her with comfort as well as a new confidence in praying. Thus she wrote in her journal:

> 'I went up . . . & Looking out of the window thought every part [of the parish] look^d dreary and dismal . . . it seemed I should have much of the cross & not be suffitient [*sic*] for the parts I was called to act in. [B]ut as I was looking to the Lord those words . . . came with

39. AMBF, MARC, FTC, MAM Fl. 23/1 p. 27; underlining in the original.

40. AMBF, MARC, FTC, MAM Fl. 23/2/1, p. 3; italics mine.

41. Cf. Mary Bosanquet Fletcher, 'Habitation', D. Frudd and T. Muck, eds. *The Asbury Journal* 61:2 (Fall 2006), 50-51. This sermon was preached on 28 March 1802. MARC, FTC, MAM Fl. 25. In a sermonic letter to Mrs. Dalby of Castle-Donington, Leicestershire, 27 August 1793, Mary Bosanquet Fletcher exegeted 1 Chron. 4:10, outlining five cries 'to the God of Israel to enlarge your coast; to bring you into that rest which remains for the people of God', including prayer, understanding, spiritual affections, [spiritual] gifts, and faith. Published in the *Wesleyan Methodist Magazine* (1818), 688-690.

42. For examples of clergymen who came to sit under her preaching, see MARC, FTC, MAM Fl. 1/4/1,5,6; 5/7/10; 5/8/3; 37/2/1-4.

double underline power to my mind, 'dont be frightened god will make you a comfortable *habitation.*' . . . & at this time I can say <u>He doth make me a comfortable *habitation.*</u> . . . I know <u>no want</u>, have full scope to use all my little talants in the work of God, no man forbiding me. My time is wholy my own, the people simple and quiet. . . . the other day some things presented of a tender kind among the pious industrious poor—I could not help asking the Lord <u>if</u> he saw good <u>a little</u> to *inlarge my borders* for their sake.[43]

Three aspects of Mary Fletcher's appropriation of promises represented by an eschatological association with 'foreigners and strangers' appear in this brief passage: (1) A sense of calling to a habitation within which to act, (2) reflection on her sphere of action, especially the note that 'no man' forbids her, and (3) the request for a greater enlargement still, not for her own benefit, but that she might enter the cycle again, using her resource for the sake of others. Eternity was always near, always insinuating itself into the present through biblical images of promises to 'strangers and foreigners of the past', and providing hope for the future.

Woe Be it Unto Me

In addition to the three images just surveyed, one other aspect of Mary's focus on eternity was important to her own sense of calling. She first began her preaching ministry in Yorkshire, and much has been written regarding this period of her life, especially in relation to her discourse with John Wesley and the network of women preachers with whom she collaborated.[44] However, one intrinsically eschatological aspect of her call to preach which has not been emphasized, is the 'prophetic' nature of that call. Women employed numerous rhetorical strategies to justify their call to preach, and Mary Fletcher's letter to Wesley in 1771 has become a model for understanding such polemics in the eighteenth century. She wrote this apologetic for women preaching in a dialogical style, listing objections followed by her defence. After refer-

---

43. Journal of Mary Fletcher, 6 January 1795, MARC, FTC, MAM Fl. 39/5/71; underlining in the original, italics mine.

44. See E.K. Brown, *Women of Mr. Wesley's Methodism* (New York, NY, 1983); Chilcote, *John Wesley*; D. Johnson, *Women in English Religion 1700-1925* (New York, NY, 1983).

ring to a substantial list of biblical examples of women preachers, prophets, and exhorters, she stated the following objection made to her along with her reply:

> Ob[jection]: but all these were Extraordinary Calls; sure[ly] you will not say yours is an Extraordinary Call?
> An[swer]: If I did not believe so I would not act in an Extraordinary manner. I do not believe Every woman is called to speak no more than Every man to be a Methodist preacher yet some have an Extraordinary Call to it & *woe be to them if they obey it not*.[45]

There are many important aspects to her letter, but we are interested here with her statement, 'woe be to them if they obey it not.' Mary's reference to 'them' includes herself, thus invoking the language and diction of the Old Testament prophets with whom she was so familiar.[46] By soliciting prophetic language, she was drawing authority for her own preaching ministry both by aligning herself with the prophetic tradition and calling to mind the final judgment where she would be held accountable. This polemic was not unprecedented, and is strikingly similar to the letter Susanna Wesley wrote to her husband, Samuel, defending her teaching ministry in his parish. Susanna wrote:

> I cannot but look upon every soul you leave under my care as a talent committed to me under a trust by the great Lord . . . And if I am unfaithful to him or to you in neglecting to improve these talents, how shall I answer to him, when he shall command me to render an account of my stewardship? . . . If you do after all think fit to dissolve this assembly . . . send me your positive command in such full and express terms as may absolve me from all guilt and punishment for neglecting this opportunity of doing good to souls, when you and I shall appear before the great and awful tribunal of our Lord Jesus Christ.[47]

45. Letter draft of Mary Fletcher to John Wesley, 1771. MAM Fl. 13/1/67, italics mine.

46. Boxes 9-10 of the FTC in the MARC contain hundreds of Mary Bosanquet Fletcher's notes on scripture, including detailed studies of the prophetic books.

47. Letter of Susanna Wesley to Samuel Wesley, Sr., 6 February 1711/12, in *Susanna Wesley: The*

Such prophetic language was not just a fear for oneself, but for lost souls due to the disobedience of the preacher. The orientation of women's prophetic utterance toward the future culmination of the kingdom of God facilitated women's justification of their prophesying by representing themselves, like the fictional Dinah Morris, as 'channels for God's spirit'. This prophetic sense of Mary Fletcher's calling was not lost on her future husband, John Fletcher, the renowned vicar of Madeley. He wrote to her regarding her ministry in 1779:

> I hope you continue stedfast, immoveable, always abounding in the work of the Lord; wiping off, by the <u>deepest humility</u>, the <u>appearance</u> of boldness and pride, which grates upon some men, when they see and hear a woman prophesying. And God fill you, and your friends, with such <u>meekness of wisdom</u>, and such <u>power from on high</u>, as may testify, that in Christ there is neither male nor female; that even Apostles may have fellow-helpers of your sex; and that the new testament, which encreases and multiplies the blessings granted under the old, has not repealed the blessings granted in the infancy of the church to Deborah, Miriam, Hannah, Hulda, and Judith.'[48]

John Fletcher's affirmation was thus proffered. Before he died in 1785, he had urged Mary to remain in the parish after his death to continue the ministry they had shared.[49] His death caused her great sorrow, but a number of dreams and visions of her late husband visiting her and conveying messages prompted her to persevere in the call to ministry in Madeley.[50] Indeed, from 1785 to her death in 1815, her ministry expanded and she functioned in many ways as a *de facto* incumbent—appointing curates, establishing religious societies and classes, catechizing children and adults, and preaching extensively.[51] During the years following his death, Mary wrote a treatise entitled *Thoughts*

Complete Writings, C. Wallace Jr., ed. (New York, NY, 1997), 79-83.

48. Letter of John Fletcher to Mary Bosanquet, 12 February 1779, MARC, MAR A.19 (a).

49. MARC, FTC, MAM Fl. 23/4/2, p. 15.

50. Many of these dreams are published in Moore, *Life of Mrs. Fletcher*. For analysis of these dreams as part of self-transcendence and agency, see Mack, *Heart Religion*, esp. chapter 6.

51. MARC, FTC, MAM Fl. 23/1-4; MAM Fl. 14.

on Communion with Happy Spirits.[52] In this work, which draws upon images of 'strangers and pilgrims' as well as the Old Testament prophets, we can see more fully the extent of Mary Fletcher's eschatological orientation in pursuing her calling. Her argument in her treatise is not only for the existence of the spirits of those who are saved after death, but their ability to communicate with those still living. There is not space here to fully explore the work, but we will look briefly at one important element which was significant in bolstering her sense of calling. Once again, drawing upon the Old Testament prophets, in the first part of her argument, the text presents the biblical story of Elisha's succession of Elijah wherein Elisha requests a 'double portion' of Elijah's prophetic spirit[53] as an example of the communion of spirits. However, the subtext reveals her own appropriation of such a request, positing that Elisha had not requested merely a 'double portion of holiness'. Her exposition offered an alternative explanation:

> [m]ight he [Elisha] not mean, let me have the two portions of thy spirit, not only thy communion with God, but let my intellectual sight be opened as thine. Let me also discern the heavenly company wherewith we are surrounded, and commune with the holy spirits of just men made perfect. . .[54]

Although it is uncertain whether she finished this work before or after she began having visitations from her late husband in dreams, by claiming to have had such visitations at all, she was appropriating a 'double portion' for herself, in that the second portion, as she exposited it, was required in order to have such discernment in the first place. As Phyllis Mack has suggested, Mary's 'dreams of her beloved dead were important to her as signs of the world beyond the grave and of her own visionary authority.'[55] She was not alone in wanting such a double portion, and several men wrote to her ex-

---

52. This was published without a publication date as an independent work (Birmingham: William Rickman King, n.d.). Moore incorporated the work into his edition of the *Life of Mrs. Fletcher*, 2:3-25. The manuscript editions in Mary's own hand are at MARC, FTC, MAM Fl. 12/2/10 and 12/3/2.

53. II Kings 2:9.

54. Moore, *Life of Mrs. Fletcher*, 2:8; 'company wherewith . . . surrounded', Heb. 12:1; 'the just made perfect', Heb. 12:23.

55. Mack, *Heart Religion*, chapter 6.

pressing their hope that her late husband's spirit would rest on them.[56] It was, at least for some, this Elisha-like double portion which Mary Fletcher had received, that contributed to her authority to preach and carry out her calling in the parish for thirty years following her husband's death.[57] Mary Fletcher found strength for her call in a focus on eternity and found comfort in her association with the 'strangers and pilgrims' who had gone before her and who then surrounded her where 'so slender did the veil appear which divides the Church militant from that which is triumphant'.[58]

Conclusion

This study of Mary Fletcher's belief in the afterlife confirms Phyllis Mack's suggestion that self-transcendence and agency were not mutually exclusive.[59] However, even though Mary saw her 'borders enlarged' and her ministry sustained, there were certainly those, like the fictional preacher Dinah Morris, who gave up preaching except for 'talking to the people a bit in their houses'[60] after the Methodist Conference in 1803 restricted women's preaching to extraordinary cases, and then, only to other women.[61] Indeed, there was great divergence in where women found authority for their preaching, and whether such authority could sustain their call. Focus on eternal things could promote self-transcendence and agency but only as a component of a complex of other beliefs and factors. More study is needed, for instance, on how the eighteenth century concept of 'family' could be melded with images of the Church to promote an extension of women's religious roles in a larger

56. For example, the Wesleyan itinerant, Thomas Rutherford (1752-1806), was caused to cry out upon receiving a gift related to her late husband, 'Lord let a double portion of his spirit rest upon me!' Letter of T. Rutherford to Mary Fletcher, 17 January 1786, MARC, FTC, MAM Fl. 6/1/21.

57. Ibid.

58. Moore, *Life of Mrs. Fletcher*, 1:69.

59. Phyllis Mack, 'Religious Dissenters in Enlightenment England', *History Workshop Journal* 49 (2000), 19-20.

60. Eliot, *Adam Bede*, 589.

61. Conference was held in Manchester from 25-30 July 1803. See *Minutes of the Methodist Conferences*, vol. 2 (London: Thomas Cordeaux, 1813), 147-189; Chilcote, *John Wesley*, 236-237, 259 n. 59. N.B. Henry Rack's comment that the Conference statement was not a ban on women's preaching, but rather represented a compromise resulting in the restricted sphere of women's preaching. Rack, 'Some Recent Trends', 197.

sphere. This essay has focused on Mary Fletcher's own sense of calling and not on how people responded to her or her apologetics. Thus, even though we know that her ministry was sustained for over fifty years, more study is needed to analyze the responses to such eschatological apologetics.

ABOUT THE MANCHESTER WESLEY
RESEARCH CENTRE

The Manchester Wesley Research Centre (MWRC) was formally inaugurated on 18 June 2003 at a service held at Nazarene Theological College (NTC), Didsbury, Manchester, England, as the concluding event of the major international conference, 'John Wesley, Life, Legend & Legacy' hosted by The University of Manchester. The Centre exists to support research in the life and work of John and Charles Wesley, their contemporaries in the eighteenth-century Evangelical Revival, their historical and theological antecedents, their successors in the Wesleyan tradition, and contemporary scholarship in the Wesleyan and Evangelical tradition. The MWRC is a collaborative partnership, drawing together a range of distinguished institutions: Asbury Theological Seminary, Wilmore, Kentucky, USA; Cliff College, Calver, England; the John Rylands Library, Manchester; Nazarene Theological College, Manchester; Nazarene Theological Seminary, Kansas City, Missouri, USA; Point Loma Nazarene University, San Diego, California, USA; and Religions and Theology at The University of Manchester. Each partner is already actively engaged in research in this field, and the object of the collaboration is to develop a centre for research with a national and international profile. Scholarly interaction is promoted by the Centre's annual sponsorship of one or more visiting research fellows for an extended period of research in Manchester. The Centre also hosts student-led research colloquiums and an annual lecture by a leading scholar in Wesley Studies.

The MWRC draws together a range of resources for researchers: the NTC library (containing nearly 50,000 items), the vast resource of the John Rylands University Library, including the Methodist Archives and Research Centre (MARC). One of the strengths of the MWRC is its growing collection of Ph.D. theses and dissertations in Wesley Studies, which complements the extensive manuscript and printed collections of the MARC.

The MWRC will sponsor two major scholarly events in 2009. With the Oxford Centre for Methodism and Church History the MWRC will co-sponsor an international conference 'Religion, Gender, Industry: Exploring Church and Methodism in a Local Setting' from 16-18 June in Madeley and Ironbridge, Shropshire. This conference will bring together authorities in the areas of church history (Methodist, Anglican and other), theology and gender studies, with social and industrial historians as well as local historians from Shropshire to examine Madeley parish. Its vicar between 1760-1785 was the Revd John Fletcher, best known as an associate of the Wesleys, but with wider evangelical links. His widow, Mary Fletcher, continued to minister in the parish until her death in 1815, a rare example of female ministry. This conference will be followed by the Fifth MWRC Annual Lecture by Professor Bruce Hindamrsh, James M. Houston Professor of Spiritual Theology at Regent College, Vancouver, on early evangelical spirituality. The lecture will take place on Friday 19 June at the J.B. Maclagan Chapel on the campus of Nazarene Theological College.

Further information about the MWRC can be obtained by visiting its web site (www.mwrc.ac.uk).

CONTRIBUTORS

HENRY D. RACK is Bishop Fraser Senior Lecturer Emeritus, The University of Manchester. He is the author of Reasonable Enthusiast: John Wesley and the Rise of Methodism.

JOSEPH W. CUNNINGHAM is a research student at Nazarene Theological College. He is writing a thesis entitled 'Perceptible Inspiration: A Model for John Wesley's Pneumatology'.

J. RUSSELL FRAZIER is a research student at Nazarene Theological College. He is writing a thesis entitled 'Living in Trinity: John Fletcher's Doctrine of Dispensations'.

RANDALL D. McELWAIN is a research student at Nazarene Theological College. He is writing a thesis entitled 'Doctrine in the Hymns of Charles Wesley: The 1780 Hymnbook as a Guide to Three Theological Themes of Early Wesleyan Methodism'.

D. R. WILSON is a research student at The University of Manchester. He is writing a thesis entitled 'Church and Chapel: Parish Ministry and Methodism in Madeley, c. 1760-1815, with Special Reference to the Ministry of John and Mary Fletcher'.

Printed in the United Kingdom by
Lightning Source UK Ltd., Milton Keynes
140388UK00001B/35/P